STUFF A GIRL'S GOTTA KNOW

Stuff a Girl's *Gotta* Know

Little Hints for the Big Things in a Girl's Life

ANDREA STEPHENS

SERVANT PUBLICATIONS
ANN ARBOR, MICHIGAN

Vine Books is an imprint of Servant Publications especially designed to serve evangelical Christians.

Servant Publications—Mission Statement
We are dedicated to publishing books that spread the gospel of Jesus Christ, help Christians to live in accordance with that gospel, promote renewal in the church, and bear witness to Christian unity.

Unless otherwise stated, all Scripture quotes are taken from *The Living Bible*, copyright 1971. Used by permission of Tyndale House Publishers, Inc., Wheaton, Ill. 60189. All rights reserved. Scripture quotations marked NAS are from the New American Standard Bible, copyright The Lockman Foundation 1960, 1962, 1963, 1968, 1971, 1972, 1973, 1975, 1977.

Servant Publications
P.O. Box 8617
Ann Arbor, MI 48107
www.servantpub.com

Cover design: PAZ Design Group, Salem, Ore.

03 04 05 06 10 9 8 7 6 5 4 3 2 1

Printed in the United States of America
ISBN 1-56955-297-5

Library of Congress Cataloging-in-Publication Data

Stephens, Andrea.
  Stuff a girl's gotta know : little hints for the big things in a
girl's life / Andrea Stephens.
      p. cm.
  ISBN 1-56955-297-5 (alk. paper)
  1. Teenage girls--Religious life. I. Title.
  BV4551.3 .S74 2003
  248.8'33--dc21
                                                    2002015561

This book is dedicated to all the teen girls
who have attended "The BABE Seminar"!

Here's a bunch more stuff you need to know
that I couldn't quite squeeze into the day!

It will help you to be focused, be strong,
and be courageous as you shine for Jesus!
And remember ...
honor God and He will honor you!

Contents

Just Gotta Say Thanks

A big *gracias* to the precious women who contributed their thoughts and expertise to these pages. Thanks for sharing your wisdom and insights with every girl who reads this book! All of you—Barbra, Lynette, Nancy, Caroline, Erika, Cari, Margaret, Tonya, Nancy, Natalie, Lisa, Stephanie, Kristie, and Katie—are my heroes!

A heartfelt thanks to Cathy Bloxham for graciously jumping in at the eleventh hour to prepare this manuscript. You have blessed me!

And to my family, friends, and prayer partners at First Presbyterian Church, who faithfully prayed for me during this project, I appreciate your endless support as I strive to be faithful to the ministry that God has called me to fulfill!

Much love,
Andrea

Intro to All This Stuff

Hey, girl!

Wow! There are only about sixteen zillion things you've gotta know! There's puberty stuff, priority stuff, popularity stuff, parent stuff, Prince Charming stuff, purity stuff, prayer stuff ... it's endless! Naturally, I couldn't jam it *all* onto these pages. However, the stuff included here will help to get you clued in on making the most of the stuff that happens in your life!

If you're like most teen girls I know, you like to talk and have lots to say. So here's a suggestion. Get yourself a spiral notebook—about the same size as this book—and jot down your responses and reactions to the stuff you read. Make notes about ideas you want to incorporate into your life, the insights you are gleaning, the things you want to change, the attitudes that you need to adjust, the opinions with which you agree (and even those you don't), and the ideas, thoughts, and feelings that are stirred by what you've read.

While you're at it, why not choose several Scriptures to memorize, and why not make note of some Bible passages you want to go back to study? And how about writing out your prayers? This will help you keep track of your conversations with God and will allow you to look back and see how He has answered your requests. That's a great faith booster!

Interacting with the text by using a journal will help you get more out of the time you invest in this book.

God bless you as you read this stuff you've gotta know, and as you grow into the beautiful young woman He has created you to be! Dive in!

Your Friend,
Andrea Stephens

Girl Stuff

From Clear Skin to Cliques to Clothes to Confidence,
Here's Some Stuff You Gotta Know About Being a Girl!

Growing Into Your Look

A huge tear, the size of a giant raindrop, made its way down Chrissie's hot cheek. She hated mornings like this. Her mom would be beeping the horn any second, she still had to gather last night's homework into her book bag, and she had no clue where her lunch ticket was hiding itself. Knowing she needed to kick it into high gear, she felt panicked, staring at the freeze-frame in front of her.

Stringy, straight hair. Pudgy cheeks. A nose like Granddad's. Absolutely no sign of breasts. And what could be worse—the hint of hair on her upper lip.

"Lord, couldn't you have done any better than this?" she weakly whispered, not sure if she really wanted Him to hear. At the sound of her mom's horn, she wiped the wetness from her face, flipped off the light, and headed out for another day.

Have you ever felt like Chrissie? Have you ever wished your appearance was slightly altered?

I can identify with her big-time!

When I was a young teen, my naturally curly hair was completely out of control. I had a Grand Canyon–sized gap between my two front teeth. My nose was so small people wondered how I could breathe. And I know all about being breastless. I didn't need a bra—I needed Band-Aids!

Then it happened.

The Big P! Yep, that's puberty!

Things started bursting and budding, lengthening and widening. And that's exactly what was supposed to occur.

Did you know that from the onset of puberty, it takes at least a full four years for your body to reach its final stage of development? I know you were hoping to be an overnight sensation, but sit tight. Be patient. Face the facts. You have to *grow* into your look!

Yes, you have your basic features in place, but between the ages of ten and twenty (the exact timing is not up to you, it's up to God) there will be a window of time when everything changes to some degree.

Let's get specific.

Growth gains. With or without your permission, your hormones leap out of hibernation, your period starts, and your body begins to grow at a faster pace as you change from a young girl to a young woman. During this time, your bones become longer and denser, and usually not all at the same time! Your arms might get ahead of your legs. Or your feet might shoot out two sizes before you get any taller. That's why most girls go through an awkward, uncoordinated phase. Fear not. Everything will catch up!

Facial features flourish. As your face works itself into its perfect proportions, all sorts of stuff takes place. Your cheekbones widen and your jawbones lengthen. Both of these changes affect the looks of your eye and nose areas. There may also be slight changes in your brow bone and forehead. All of this works together as you take on a more mature look.

Upper body blossoms. OK, finally! Your nipples begin to push out from your chest as the mammary glands develop beneath them. Breasts appear! One may appear sooner than the other, but they will eventually even out. You probably need to check out the bra department as soon as you begin budding. To avoid embarrassing nipple moments, select a bra (and bathing suit top) with a thicker cup—not super padded, but more than a single layer.

Carve out the curves. Now let's talk lower body. Your pelvic bone widens, causing your hips and thighs to fill out. No! You are not getting fat! God has programmed the female figure to be fleshy for the purpose of child-bearing (later in life, like after the honeymoon). Apparently, girls who are hard on themselves or tease others about teenage weight gain are ignorant of God's plan.

Hair happenings. Soft hair appears on various parts of your body, like your underarms, legs, pubic area, chest, upper lip, between your eye-brows, maybe even on your big toes! Don't worry ... all of this is normal. Your beautiful head of hair might hold more oil during this time. Shampoo daily and occasionally apply conditioner to the ends of your hair.

Perspiration princess. Your sweat glands get geared up and start work-ing overtime. Some girls perspire or have more odor than others. Sweat is actually good; it gets rid of harmful toxins. To prevent yourself from being plagued with an undesirable aroma, shower daily and arm your-self with an antiperspirant and deodorant protection (remember, antiperspirants stop wetness, deodorants stop odor). Then splash on your favorite fragrance.

All of these changes are part of the totally cool, complex, ingenious Master-minded workings of the human body. They are normal and nat-ural. They take you from childhood into adulthood, giving you a look that is yours alone! You are a custom-designed diva!

Pop Apart That Popularity Puzzle

One of the most stressful things in a girl's life is the popularity thing. Does it ever feel puzzling to you? Sometimes it seems like there's some unwritten rule about *how* to be popular and *who* can be popular. And just when you think you've got a piece of the puzzle figured out, the whole thing changes!

I chatted with a few of my teen friends about this connection craziness. Scoot a little closer. I invite you to eavesdrop.

JEN: Just hearing the word stresses me. When I think of all the phoniness that goes along with popularity, I want to be sick. Some girls want everyone to like them, so they try to be what others want them to be and they totally lose who *they* are. Being part of the clique is highly overrated!

LISA: Yeah. It's so much better to be real and be honest. Just be yourself, not a fake.

JEN: Like Cindy. She's popular, but it's because she *is* herself. She's confident and funny and encouraging to others. She fits with lots of people. I love it when she shows up at student council meetings with her slippers on. At least she didn't wear them on Homecoming Court.

JORDIE: After watching the problems of most of the popular kids at my school, I don't *want* to be popular. It's my choice. I don't want the pressures that go along with being in the "in" group.

Little Hint

Look around. Based on our society's unrealistic beauty standards, most girls are not supermodel material. Yet, every girl is gorgeous in *God's* eyes. That includes you! You are handcrafted by the Master Designer! Learn to love your appearance by appreciating your uniqueness.

BETH: I know what you mean. I have a few close friends, not a lot, but at least I know they really are *true* friends. They are always there for me, even when I'm having a grouchy day.

LISA: I always wanted to be popular, but I'm with Beth. It's better to know I have some true friends and that I'm popular with them.

EMILY: I felt popular while I was dating Matt. Since he was a football player, we got invited to lots of parties and stuff. It felt good to have some of those people actually talk to me. But once Matt dumped me for Kim, not one of those people talked to me anymore. Plus, I used to think I was missing out on something really great when I wasn't invited to anything. Now I know the parties are no big deal. Kids are drinking, getting high, and pairing off in bedrooms. That's not what I want. There's better stuff in life than getting caught up in all that.

JORDIE: I think popularity sets up unfair measuring sticks, like you are not worth much if you don't rate with certain students or meet some standard. That stinks. A person is not more valuable just because she has tons of friends or the "right" friends.

BETH: I agree. Our value is not based on whether or not other people like us. It's based on God. He values us, therefore each of us is valuable.

JEN: When you look at it that way, I guess you could say we are all popular. We're popular with God! He knows us and likes us! We're not "average," because nobody is average to God!

EMILY: Yeah, that's so cool.

Cool, indeed!

Don't try to act big. Don't try to get into the good graces of important people, but enjoy the company of ordinary folks.

ROMANS 12:16

Sensible Steps to Fresh-Looking Skin

The occasional acne attack is inevitable, but here are some ways to keep your skin clean and clear. Yet before you start washing, scrubbing, or lavishing your skin with lotion, you need to know which products to use. How do you know that? By identifying your skin type!

Take this simple test:

 Before you turn out the lights and call it a night, cleanse your face. Do not apply anything to your skin (no astringent, no lotion). The next day, as soon as you wake up, lay a piece of tissue paper over your entire face. Now press the tissue against your skin at your forehead, cheeks, the sides of your nose, and the middle of your chin. Lift the tissue, holding it up to the light. A slight bit of oil indicates normal skin; no oil means you have dry skin; lots of oil is a sure sign of oily skin. If you are oily in one spot and dry in another, you are the proud owner of beautiful combination skin. Actually, most teens are oily in the T-zone. Yep, that's across the forehead and down the center of the face!

Carefully read labels and choose products designed for your skin type. When it comes to skin care, use products from the same company, because they have been designed to work together. Look for allergy-tested, fragrance-free, non-comedogenic (won't clog pores) brands that have been stripped of ingredients that cause redness, rashes, breakout, burning, or itching.

Cleanse! First things first: Keeping your skin fresh and clear requires double duty—once in the morning, once in the evening (never go to bed with your makeup on)! Cleanse your face with a nondetergent bar, lotion, or gel. Work up a sudsy lather while moving your fingertips in a circular motion. Your facial skin and muscles are very delicate, so avoid pulling, rubbing, or pressing hard. Rinse the cleanser off using luke-warm water, then gently pat your face dry with a clean towel.

Tone! Next, dab some astringent or toner on a fluffy 100 percent cotton ball, and apply it to your face. Use a circular motion all the way up to your hairline and under your chin, steering clear of your eye area. Astringent or toner will help to slough off dead skin cells (a process technically known as exfoliation) and remove excess oil.

Moisturize! Last but not least, treat your skin to the soft, smoothing effects of moisturizer. This will seal in natural fluids and replace moisture your skin loses due to sun, wind, perspiration, artificial air conditioning/heating, and pollution. All skin types need moisture! Those with normal to dry skin can select a heavier moisturizer, while those with normal to oily skin should go with an oil-free type. And don't forget your precious lips! Glide on some lip balm to soften and prevent chapping. Hey, you can even choose one in your favorite flavor, like cherry, wild berry, or orange! Yum!

 It's TLC time! Occasionally your skin is going to need some tender loving care. Try these tips to make it feel special:

♥   Drink six to eight glasses of water each day to cleanse your skin from the inside out. Sodas and lattes don't count!

♥   Every day apply a lotion with an SPF of 15 or higher to protect your skin from the harmful rays of the sun. Apply it right after your moisturizer, or use a moisturizer or foundation that already has the sunscreen mixed in!

♥ Once or twice a week, open up your pores with a bowl of steaming water or by pressing a wet, warm washcloth against your face for two to four minutes. Then splash with lukewarm water—about ten times. Now apply a facial scrub to chase away any dull-looking skin. Choose one made with tiny round beads, not ground up fruit pits! Rinse with warm water.

♥ When you have an acne attack, switch to a cleanser or toner that contains salicylic acid. Then apply a product with benzoyl peroxide directly on zits to kill bacteria and speed up the healing process. If these over-the-counter zit zappers aren't giving you the results you want, go to your local dermatologist for help. All acne can be treated.

Are You Feeding Your Emotions?

Jill's mom reminded her three times to make her bed and wash the previous night's dinner dishes before leaving the house. Yet after fixing her hair and ironing her new shirt, Jill was running late. The honking horn from Anna's car only made the pressure worse. So out she dashed, her bedspread still sprawled on the floor and the dinner plates still stacked in the sink, hardened with spaghetti. Hours later, Jill returned home to an irritated mother who grounded her for two weeks. Jill was instantly ticked. She headed for the kitchen and made herself a King Kong-sized hot fudge sundae, trying to eat her anger away.

* * *

It was Saturday night, and Nan was home alone with a mint-green clay mask on her face. Who could've guessed her skin would have erupted with pimples last Thursday? So Nan was having a pity party and watching old movies while her friends were out having fun. Feeling very sad and lonely, she cried rivers of tears and ate loads of chips, buttered popcorn, and cheesy nachos, hoping to lift her spirits.

*　　*　　*

Erica had panicked big-time over her history exam. Trying to sort out and memorize the dates and places of historical events had taxed her brain. Yet the test hadn't seemed as hard as she'd expected. Scanning for her name on the bulletin board where grades were posted, Erica felt a knot of anticipation. Scholl, Smithers, Snead—there it was. Her eyes widened in disbelief; her heart jumped. A 92 percent! Time to celebrate! She headed toward the vending machine and treated herself to some big, soft, chocolate chip cookies. She stopped for gas on the way home and continued her rejoicing with a bag of M&M's. At home she polished off two bagels loaded with cream cheese. Nothing like a good pig-out to reward herself.

*　　*　　*

Jill was mad. Nan was sad. Erica was glad. Yet all three girls responded to their feelings with *food!* While food can provide a temporary satisfaction, it usually leads to drowsiness, skin breakouts, and eventually, excess weight gain.

Emotions are fickle things, especially for girls. However, using food to deal with them is not your best bet. Before you get caught in this routine, check out these constructive ways to feed your emotions and work through your feelings.

When you're *mad* ... Anger is often involuntary. Something happens, and before you know it, you're mad. Yet anger can be lethal if allowed to grow. So, stomp out the spark before it becomes a flaming fire. How? By forgiving whoever made you angry. Whether it's yourself, your parents, or one of your friends, *let it go!* Holding a grudge is not an option. God says we are to be slow to anger and quick to forgive (even if we're not at fault). Is there anyone *you* need to forgive?

When you're *sad* ... Having the blues is a normal part of the ups and downs of life. But *staying* down and depressed is not. Try talk therapy! Find a mature Christian—someone you trust—and let it all out. No one to talk to? Then write it out. Start a journal. Make a habit of writing when things start piling up on the inside. God is always there to listen. Is there anything *you* need to talk about?

When you're *glad* ... When you're happy, treat yourself to the extra rewards that come from sharing your cheerfulness. Try writing to your grandparents or to friends and telling them your good news. Take your happy attitude to an elderly neighbor or a nursing home. You'll be doubly blessed when you spread some love and excitement their way. Use your joy to brighten someone else's world. Who could you share *your* good mood with today?

Little Hint

Challenge yourself to eat three to five fresh fruits and one to two cups of raw, uncooked veggies daily. Then add three servings of cooked veggies, three to five servings of grains (cereal, rice, oats, pasta), and some good protein sources like chicken, turkey, soy, yogurt, or low-fat cottage cheese! Healthy eating can enhance healthy emotions!

Flirty Fashions

I love fashion. Always have, probably always will.

In high school I made lots of my own clothes because I never wanted to be dressed exactly like anyone else. Sewing allowed me to select my own fabrics, colors, and designs.

My love for fashion led me to take fashion design classes during my first year of college. The next summer I landed a contract with Wilhelmina Models, Inc. and moved to New York City. It was only like *the* fashion capital of the USA! I was elated!

Now, several years later (OK, many years later), I still love clothes. If there's a Nordstrom or Saks Fifth Avenue within fifty miles, I'll sniff it out. If there is a Talbots in the area, I'm there!

Yet my addiction goes beyond the high-priced palaces with designer names.

Give me Wal-Mart, give me Target.

I might be there to pick up some mascara or get some film developed, but a stroll through the clothing section is usually in the back of my brain!

So, I admit it.

I'm a fashionholic.

I want to be in style. Yet the styles no longer dictate my selections.

Here's the thing. In my younger years, I realized that some of the clothes I wore—especially the ones that made me *feel* sort of stylish—seemed to be attracting attention. The *wrong* kind. It was as if the fashions themselves were flirting.

See, there are these creatures called boys. Guys. Males. God wired them totally differently than He wired us females. Yes, we're talking physically here! Usually, guys start feeling attracted to girls based on sight! What they *see* affects their sexual appetites.

Gosh.

There's an appetite I didn't (and still don't) want to feed!

I found that short skirts, barely-there tops, and form-fitting fashions lured the guys my way, but it was for all the wrong reasons. No, I wasn't trying to get their attention (though I liked it a little), but still, even if my intentions were innocent and fashion-driven, I got the same reaction as the girl who purposely dressed seductively.

I didn't want a guy to be drawn to me for my body.

Neither did fifteen-year-old Kimberly, who recently told me that this guy at school kept making sexual comments to her. At first she didn't know why. "I'm not that kind of girl," she explained. Yet when she stopped and analyzed the situation, she realized that she didn't dress any differently than the girls who *were* "that kind of girl." She knew some changes were in order.

And so did I.

See, when a guy is attracted to a girl for purely physical reasons, it always gets a relationship started off on the wrong path. Truthfully, what girl wants a guy who is interested in only her body? Wouldn't it be better to attract the attention of a beau because of your winsome personality, your academic achievements, your athletic abilities, your friendliness, your inner beauty? Yes! My teen friend Marissa says she saves herself a lot of grief by dressing differently. She doesn't have to worry about bending over and showing cleavage, doesn't have to be tugging constantly on her miniskirt when she sits down, and doesn't have to be concerned that a guy asks her out just to get her in the backseat of his car. She has lots of guy friends because that sexual tension is not there.

So, my first real fashion crisis came not when I couldn't figure out what to wear to prom or to a fancy dinner date, but when I realized I couldn't wear just absolutely anything I wanted. Even though clothes are an avenue of self-expression, I realized I would need to learn to express myself a little differently.

I also realized that I didn't want to lead anyone astray or cause anyone to stumble by what I was wearing. Since guys are aroused by sight,

I didn't want to cause someone to have impure and ungodly thoughts.

There are several Bible verses that speak directly to this topic. (The Bible has a way of doing that—it's so practical!) Romans 14:13 and Matthew 18:6 both speak of *not* causing another person to stumble, meaning to sin.

Then there is Hebrews 10:24, "And let us consider how to stimulate one another to love and good deeds" (NAS). Since good deeds start with good thoughts, could that mean that if we cover up a bit more we could steer a guy's thoughts away from "going there"?

Could that mean we have a responsibility to help our brothers in Christ (and guys in general) to maintain pure thoughts by dressing modestly—you know, less revealing?

Hey, wait. Isn't it the guy's responsibility to maintain self-control? Yes, but we can help them out by choosing to wear clothes that don't attract so much attention to our bodies.

The key word here is *choose*.

I had a choice to make when I faced my fashion crisis years ago. I still make that same choice every time I hit the mall. Perhaps you have a choice to make, too.

Girls, are we willing to:
- ♥ sacrifice our fashion flair to be obedient to God's Word?
- ♥ refuse to be a potential stumbling block to guys?
- ♥ be more interested in inner substance than in style?
- ♥ be a godly example instead of building a trendy wardrobe?
- ♥ be OK with not "fitting in" with what lots of other girls are wearing?

I pray you will join in wholeheartedly, and answer with a resounding "Yes!" (OK, even if it's not wholehearted, follow your head and your feelings will catch up eventually).

Now, does all of this mean that we have to be fashion duds?

No way! Not even close!

There are a ton more ways to be stylish than wearing the teeniest trends! I know it can be a challenge, since many clothing companies purposely design clothes to attract attention to one's body. But you can do it! Let's think outside the box a bit.

Ten Ways to (Still) Be Stylin'!

1. Go with a modified version of what's "hot." Instead of having clothes hug your body, try wearing them one size larger. This is potentially more comfortable, and will make you feel less self-conscious.

2. If a certain style of top is cut too low in the front, wear a tube top or tank under it. It's best to avoid strapless and halter tops. When it comes to bottoms, if you want to wear hipsters or low-rise cuts, no problem. Just top them off with a shirt that tucks in or at least touches the top of the jeans. Better yet, wear a body suit or leotard to eliminate the possibility of exposing your belly button or your backside!

3. During the cooler months, make shorter skirts more wearable by matching the color of the skirt with a pair of tights that are the same tone.

4. Choose a totally different look. There is always more than one look that is popular at the time. Of course, you can always create your own look. Instead of short skirts, go with super-long ones. Instead of capris, maybe bib overalls are more your style! Be creative! Be individual!

5. Every season, not only are there fashionable styles, there are also fashionable colors. Shop around to see what hues are

splashed throughout the stores. Then make purchases in those colors. If lemon-lime is "in" for the spring, it will look just as good in a sleeveless "T" as it will in a midriff. So, modest styles in great colors are a great alternative! Then expand the latest colors into your accessories—your sandals, sneakers, backpack, tote, purse, earrings, hair stuff, and so on.

6. Speaking of accessories, that's another way to be in style. Shoes vary each season, as do bracelets, belts, sunglasses, earrings, bandanas, rings, watches, and purses. You can update any outfit with some fun sidekicks!

7. Fabrics can be trendy, too. If ribbed silk or polyester-satin is in, great! Go for it!

8. Hairstyles are another great form of self-expression and style. Choose the style that reflects the true you!

9. There is usually a new makeup trend on the horizon. If it's not totally weird, give it a try. Nail polishes, decals, and designs can add a cool touch, too!

10. Take a stroll through the other departments in your favorite store. Why limit yourself to the junior department? You can find less trendy, yet very contemporary clothes in sportswear or missy sections.

Little Hints

♥ Shop with a like-minded friend. Hold each other accountable for dressing modestly and honoring God! After all, your body is His temple (check out 1 Corinthians 6:19-20).

♥ Use God's Word as a plumb line. This helps you to know what's OK and what's not. Use verses like Romans 12:2 to guide your decisions: Don't be conformed to the patterns of this world. Be new and different!

♥ It's true that you can buy fashionable clothes, but real style comes from within!

♥ Dressing in your own unique way may invite a variety of reactions from peers, not all of them positive. Let it go! Build your self-esteem (and your wardrobe) on God's opinion.

♥ The best-dressed girl is always wearing a smile. Choose to be "best dressed": *Smile!*

Puberty, Periods, and Pads!
Straight Talk With Physician's Assistant Erika Schroeder

I remember watching television with my family when I was younger and wouldn't you know it ... one of *those* commercials came on. It was advertising tampons. I just wanted to die! As a teenager, I felt self-conscious enough about the changes taking place within me. Why did there have to be commercials to draw attention to it? Oh, how traumatic!

During this sometimes awkward stage of womanhood, you may have questions about what is going on with your body. Hopefully the information provided here will leave you with a better understanding of the process of becoming a woman who has been beautifully designed by God!

Puberty is defined in the medical journals as "the physical, emotional, and sexual transition from childhood to adulthood." Even though puberty is a gradual process, controlled by different hormones, there are some specific events that stand out. Things like breast development, growth spurts, hair growth—you know what I mean!

Each of these things *begins* at a different time for each different girl—typically between the ages of ten and sixteen. Why at different ages? Remember that God made each of us unique. Our bodies weren't designed to develop on cue or at the same rate as those of our friends or sisters! Even though I can't exactly predict when each stage of development will take place in *you*, there are three important things that have to occur before your hormones kick in and you start developing. Here they are:

1. Body weight of 85 to 106 pounds. No matter how tall or short you are, you must reach a certain weight, and therefore a certain percentage of body fat (about 16 to 24 percent), before some of those necessary hormones even *begin* to think about working. This should be a wake-up call and a reminder to you that your body *needs* some fat in order for it to work properly! God meant for it to be there for a reason. That is why some girls who are on starvation-type diets or who exercise excessively have irregular periods—if they have a period at all.

2. Getting enough sleep. No joke! For girls who have not started their period but who have some breast development and pubic hair growth, sleep can have an effect on hormone release. That's another reason to get a good night's sleep every night!

3. Exposing your eyes to sunlight. Here's some trivia for you: Blind girls start their periods at a later age than do girls with full sight. Now if you feel like you are behind in your physical development, I'm not suggesting you bathe in the sun or bake those baby blues in a tanning bed! This is just to let you know that your body requires fresh air and sunshine.

4. Proper nutrition. It is important that you eat lots of healthy, nutritious foods, drink at least eight glasses of water per day, and take a multiple vitamin every day!

Now that we have discussed what your precious body needs to develop, let's talk about what is going to happen when you get to that point (or what has already been happening to some of you). The female reproductive cycle, which is typically twenty-eight days long, can be divided into four parts:

- Menstruation—the three to five days of bleeding that takes place during your menstrual cycle when the lining of the uterus is shedding away.
- Follicular Phase—development of an egg.
- Ovulation—when an egg is released from your ovary.
- Luteal Phase—the building up of the uterine lining.

These different parts of the cycle occur as a result of some very special hormones increasing and decreasing in your body at different times of the month (estrogen, follicle stimulating hormone, luteinizing hormone, and progesterone).

Females have two ovaries whose job is to make an egg every month. If the egg is fertilized and implants in the uterus, a precious baby is brought into the world nine months later! If the egg is not fertilized, the level of hormone called progesterone drops and tells the lining of the uterus to "disappear." This is the bleeding during your period ... that lining shedding away. Depending on your body, the bleeding usually lasts for three to five days. The amount of bleeding varies. You may have light bleeding (or spotting), while your best friend might have heavy bleeding, clots of blood, and painful cramps.

Let's talk nitty-gritty. Do you catch the blood in a pad or absorb it into a tampon? It's really personal preference! Some girls like to start with a pad, since they are easier to use. Some girls think a pad feels like wearing a diaper and therefore choose to go the tampon route. Pads feel more secure when they fit snug against your body with the help of undies made with a touch of spandex or Lycra.

Using a tampon is very convenient, especially if you are active in sports. Some are concerned that if they use a tampon, they are no longer virgins. *Not* true. The main thing to know about tampons (besides how to insert them correctly) is that you need to change them every four to six hours in order to prevent an infection.

Hey, let's do some Q & A! These are the most common questions I am asked. Chances are, you've wondered about these things, too!

Q: I am fourteen and a half years old and I haven't started my period. I'm the only one in my group of friends who hasn't. Should I be worried?

A: Don't panic just yet! Having your period isn't the only sign that you have reached womanhood. Breast development, the presence of pubic hair, and starting your period are all important parts of a girl's development. Be patient as your body develops according to its own God-given schedule! Now, if you haven't begun developing at all by the time you are fourteen, you should let your doctor know. Similarly, if you have not started your period by age sixteen, regardless of whether you have breasts and underarm or pubic hair, your doctor needs to know. With a little detective work, a physical exam, and some blood work, he or she will be able to uncover the reason your body is not in full bloom.

Q: I started my period one year ago, but lately it has been so irregular. What should I do?

A: Excessive exercising, poor diet, intense stress, and losing a lot of weight are a few common causes of irregular periods. So my question to you is ... are you eating a balanced diet? Have you recently lost weight? Are you working out too much? Is there something happening in your life that you are majorly stressed about? Give it some thought!

Some irregularity is normal when you first get your period. Your body is getting used to this womanhood thing and it won't always be like perfect clockwork at the beginning. If you are concerned, talk your situation over with your physician.

Q: What is the purpose of a pelvic exam, and how is it done?

A: The purpose of a pelvic exam is to do a cervical cancer screening called a Pap smear (a swab of cells is taken from the cervix, fixed on a slide, and then sent to a lab to be evaluated for any abnormal cells) to detect any abnormalities in the reproductive organs. It is important to have your first exam done around the age of eighteen. Risk factors for cervical cancer include: early age of first intercourse, multiple partners, sexually transmitted diseases, and smoking. The Pap smear has the ability to detect abnormal cells, so it can literally save a woman's life!

When you are going to have your first exam, the most important thing to do is *relax*. You will be taken into the exam room and asked to remove your clothes and put on a really cute paper gown (just kidding, they aren't very cute). Then you will lie back on the examination table and put your feet up into the two "stirrups." The doctor will then insert into your vagina a long plastic or metal device called a speculum. It is used to keep the vaginal area open, thus exposing the cervix (the entrance to the uterus). Then a long cotton swab or brush will be used to collect a sample of cells from the cervix. They will then be fixed on a slide and sent to a lab to be evaluated for any abnormal cells.

Then the doctor will do a manual exam with glove-covered hands to check the size and shape of the uterus and to detect any unusual masses of tissue. It will be over before you know it!

Q: Sometimes I feel moody. Is that normal?

A: Yes! During sexual maturation, you may notice that your mood changes quite a bit. This is normal, for the most part. Feelings that range from "super sad" to "happy as can be" are just another example of your body trying to deal with the cycle of hormone changes that takes place each month. Be patient with yourself during this time.

Erika Schroeder is a graduate of Pepperdine University and Baylor College of Medicine. She easily landed her first job as a physician's assistant in Bakersfield, California. She's fun, single, and loves learning new stuff in her gymnastics class!

Little Hint

God does not measure our hips; He measures our hearts!

Feeling Mellow Yellow? Perhaps It's the Blues!
Getting Personal With Margaret Koontz

Life can be tough. All sorts of things happen that can leave you feeling blue. A friend lets you down. You don't pass a test. Someone starts an unkind rumor about you. The cute guy doesn't call even though he said he would. You feel down. Who wouldn't? But you get over it, just like your mom said you would. (Don't you hate it when she's right?)

Some things are harder to get over. Your boyfriend decides to date your best friend. Your mom and dad get divorced. Your grandma dies. You're left feeling sad and empty and more than a little lonely. It takes longer to get back to feeling like yourself again. Tears are quick to fall and nothing is fun anymore. But you get up, you get dressed, you get pretty, you go to school, and after a while you find you're doing OK. (The Lord was there for you, and you had friends and family to talk to as well. They said you'd make it, and you're actually glad they were right!)

Sometimes the world gets gray and the sadness just won't go away. My son got very sick when he was twelve and spent the next five years in bed (yes, count 'em—five years—that was *all* of junior high and most of high school). There were times when both of us felt like there was no hope, no future, no solution, and nothing that would make the deep sadness go away. All but a handful of his friends forgot about him, and that added to the sadness. We prayed. We talked. We cried. We learned firsthand that there is a difference between just having the blues and being truly depressed.

Depression doesn't usually go away by itself. That's the bad news. However, the good news is that depression can be treated, usually with a good dose of faith, a shoulder to cry on, and the help of someone who understands depression and understands you. So, how do you know if it's just the blues or if you're truly depressed and going to need a little help to feel like the sun is shining again? Read through the following questions and answer them by circling "yes" or "no."

How You Can Tell

Do you feel:

Sad or anxious all of the time?	Yes	No
All empty inside?	Yes	No
Guilty or worthless?	Yes	No
Like there's no hope?	Yes	No

Are you:

Sleeping too much? Too little?	Yes	No
Losing weight because you're never hungry?	Yes	No
Gaining weight because you're always hungry?	Yes	No
All tired out with no way to get energized?	Yes	No
Grumpy or restless for no reason?	Yes	No

Are you having:

All kinds of aches and pains?	Yes	No
Headaches or other physical problems?	Yes	No
Difficulty concentrating, making decisions, remembering things?	Yes	No

Have you:

Stopped doing the things you like?	Yes	No
Stopped enjoying everyday life?	Yes	No
Stopped being around your friends?	Yes	No
Started wanting life to be over?	Yes	No

Apply the "five for two" rule. If you said "yes" to five or more of the symptoms listed above and have been having them for more than two weeks, chances are, you are struggling with depression. There are lots of things you can do to feel better.

What You Can Do

Fill your mind and heart with God's promises. The Bible is packed full of wonderful promises for you. Pull your concordance (a book that helps you locate scriptures by topic or word) off the shelf and look up words like hope, comfort, peace, joy, trustworthy, and faithful. Write the verses down on cards and tape them up everywhere: on the mirror, on your binder, on your math book, on your juice glass, on your calendar, on your toothbrush, by the telephone, and my favorite, as bookmarks for everything you're reading. Read these promises every chance you get. Say them out loud. Pick one each day and memorize it. Let God's promises fill up your heart and your mind and the sadness will have to take a big step back. God is the Great Healer, and He specializes in broken hearts and broken spirits. Let Him be your best friend and your greatest ally and bring you back to the joyful life He wants you to have.

Tell someone. You can't solve this by yourself. The people around you have probably already noticed that something is bothering you. Tell a parent or grandparent, a teacher or school counselor, your minister or youth pastor. They care and can help you find the help you need to be yourself again.

See your family doctor. Your doctor has lots of resources to help you. He or she can begin by ruling out anything else that might be wrong, like diabetes or a vitamin deficiency. Then, if an antidepressant would help get your body back into its normal rhythms, it can be prescribed.

Talk it through. One of the best cures for depression is talking it through with someone who knows how to listen. There are many good counselors who specialize in teens and will understand what you're going through. Your parents, minister, or school counselor can help you find the right one.

Get some exercise. When you take a brisk walk, bike ride, or Rollerblade, your heart rate goes up and your body releases endorphins into your bloodstream. These are your body's natural "feel good" hormones. Vigorous exercise really gives you a physiological and psychological boost!

Put these ideas into practice and your feelings of depression will lift. Trust the Lord to lead you and comfort you as down days turn into joyful days.

Margaret Koontz became a Christian when she was a teen and loves to tell others about Jesus and the new life He brings. She has taught everything from preschool music to eighth-grade history. She lives in Southern California, with her husband and two grown sons and is soon to be a mother-in-law.

Little Hint

Michael W. Smith has a song that states, "love isn't love until you give it away."

How true it is! The message behind those words is short, sweet, and very direct. Ready? Here it is: *Love is action!* Genuine love is more than a thought or a feeling. It has movement and motion. It has hands and feet. It is something that can be seen.

In observing love in action you will see that it is patient. It is kind. It is not selfish or rude. It doesn't demand its own way. It is an unconditional giving of oneself. It is, in fact, the kind of love that God extends toward us, and the kind of love He desires for us to extend toward others. He puts forth the challenge. Will our response be passive or active?

A new commandment I give to you, that you love one another, even as I have loved you, that you also love one another. By this all men will know that you are My disciples, if you have love for one another.

JOHN 13:34-35, NAS

You, as a girl, are uniquely gifted with the ability to love, to nurture, to comfort. Don't hold back. Let it flow!

Perfectly Poised!

Picture it. Contestant No. 1 trudges in, her head down, her eyes glued to the floor. She slumps into the closest chair, her shoulders drooping. She's looking sad or mad, but definitely not glad!

Contestant No. 2 glides in, strutting her stuff. Her head is up, up, up, along with her nose. Shoulders? Back—way back—causing her chest to be the center of attention. Her eyes are looking right at you—no wait, they are looking right *past* you!

Enter Contestant No. 3. Whoa. This one is smiling. Her head is held erect, but neither too far up nor down. And she's actually looking at you, right in the eyes! She walks with her shoulders slightly back, and as she gently sits down, she maintains her composed look instead of melting into the chair.

The winner? Well, who appeared confident, friendly, approachable? Who made you feel good about yourself just by being around her? Contestant No. 3, of course!

What Is It?

Posture. It is best defined as the manner in which a person carries herself. You know, the way you stand, sit, and walk. Yet posture is more than that. Posture talks. It sends a message to others about your attitude, your feelings, and your state of mind.

Wow! All of that from a person's posture? Yep! And more—it also tells us about your confidence level. Our first contestant didn't have enough confidence to fill a peanut shell. Contestant No. 2 looked like she had enough for you, me, and half the state of Texas. (Did you know that people who appear overly confident are often acting that way to hide their insecurities?)

Our winner was truly confident. She held herself well, was able to smile, and looked you in the eye. She could put others at ease. That's a sign of genuine confidence.

What About You?

Which contestant do you most resemble? Observe yourself. Stand in front of a full-length mirror. How would you describe your general posture? Are you slouching or standing straight? Is your chin up, down, or in between? Now catch your side view. Does your neck lean forward, causing your chin to jut out? Or do you hold your head back, sort of like a soldier? If you drew a straight line from your shoulder to your heel, would everything be in line, or slightly out of whack?

Have a seat. After a few minutes, are you leaning? Slouching? Sitting with your legs apart? Oh, sure. There are times when it's OK to do these things. But do you know when to use good posture and when it's all right to be relaxed?

Now that you've given yourself the once-over, what do you think? Are there a few things that need to be changed? Are you ready to do it? Will you practice new techniques, remembering that practice makes perfect? The more you use correct posture, the sooner it will become natural. You will look and feel more confident! And your body will be glad you made the changes.

That's right. Carrying yourself correctly allows more room for your inner organs and makes way for you to take deep breaths. Good posture lets more air into the diaphragm. Instead of taking shallow breaths from the upper chest area, you will be able to breathe deeply into your lower lungs. Not only is deep breathing relaxing, but the increase in oxygen is good for your health.

Good posture keeps your spine (that's the collection of twenty-six vertebrae up and down your back) straight or upright, thus minimizing pinched nerves or misalignment. Besides all this body stuff, good posture helps your clothes fit better and helps you make a favorable first impression.

So, let's stop talking and start practicing the simple steps that will lead you to be perfectly poised!

Six Points to Good Posture

1. Hold your head directly above your shoulders, keeping your chin parallel with the floor. Avoid leaning your neck forward or backward.
2. If necessary, pull your shoulders slightly back, but not up toward your ears.
3. Lift your rib cage. If you take a deep breath, you can feel it lift. It is nearly impossible for your shoulders to slump forward if your rib cage is properly lifted.

4. If you tend to stand swaybacked (with your lower spine curving outward), gently rotate your pelvic bone forward a little.

5. When standing, let your arms hang naturally at your sides. When walking, slightly swing your arms. Your palms should be facing the outer side of your thigh. Always use controlled movement—no floppy arms!

6. Let the sparkle in your eyes and the kindness in your smile be the finishing touches on your new poised appearance.

Posture Exercises

Here are two exercises to tone up the muscles you will be using with your new posture techniques.

The Spine Stretch. Stand with your feet shoulder-width apart, arms hanging by your sides. Slowly drop your head forward, allowing it to lead as you bend forward one vertebra at a time, until you are bent over as far as is comfortable. Allow your arms to hang toward the floor. Now, slowly roll yourself back up into a standing position.

Upper Back Builder. Stand in perfect-posture position. Lift your arms out to your sides, then move them backward as far as you are able to reach. Hold for fifteen seconds, relax, then repeat ten times.

Take a Stand

An important part of good posture definitely includes the way you stand. Here are two suggestions.

Side-by-side. Put your feet together, toes pointing straight ahead. Your weight should be equally balanced on both feet, which will keep you from leaning on one leg or cocking your hip as you flex one knee.

Model's stance. This is my favorite. It looks a bit more poised. Stand with your front foot pointed directly forward. Your back foot is to be at a forty-five-degree angle with the heel of your front foot touching the center of your back foot so the front knee looks relaxed.

Now that you know the secrets to perfect posture, be sure to practice, practice, practice! Soon enough these simple techniques will come naturally!

Christian Kind of Confidence

As a Christian, a precious daughter of God Himself, you have a bazillion reasons to feel confident. Yet, why take my word for it? Take God's Word.

Grab your Bible (New American Standard will work best for these) and look up these incredibly cool verses, then fill in the blanks to complete the picture of the new, confident you!

1 Peter 2:9

As a member of God's family you are part of a _____ race, a _____ priesthood, a _____ nation! You totally belong to _____ and are now living in His marvelous _____!

Wow! You are somebody special!

Ephesians 2:4-6

God _____ you so much that He made you _____ with Christ! He has even seated you with Christ in _____ places.

Wow! No need to feel low! You rank high with God!

Hebrews 4:16

Because of Jesus, you can come to God's _____ with great _____, knowing He will give you grace and _____ when you need it!

You don't have to shy away from God!

John 15:15-16

You are not a slave who doesn't know what her master is doing! Jesus has called you His _____!

Honest! He's the best one you'll ever have!

1 John 1:9

No matter what you do, when you _____ your sins, _____ will instantly _____ you!

That's good news that will keep you standing tall!

Check your answers. But hey—don't peek until you're finished filling in *all* the blanks.

1 Peter 2:9—chosen, royal, holy, God, light
Ephesians 2:4-6—loved, alive, heavenly
Hebrews 4:16—throne, confidence, mercy
John 15:15-16—friend
1 John 1:9—confess, Jesus, forgive

For the Lord will be your confidence....

Proverbs 3:26, NAS

A Look at Eating Disorders

Sarah looked like your typical girl next door. Yet inside, her fears were raging. See, when Sarah's hormones kicked in at puberty, her hips, thighs, and bust areas filled out and took on a new softness. She panicked over the changes, concluding she was fat. To her, *fat meant failure*.

Sarah began downing diet pills and bingeing—eating lots of food, then throwing up. She dropped out of band and spent all her time working out! In a short period of time Sarah was a full-fledged bulimic and became very sick. Her parents put her in a hospital for treatment. There she learned about proper nutrition and how to care for her 5'1", large-boned body that would never be 5'9" and tiny.

"I hope others never go through what I've been through. Being afraid of food and hating your body is awful—you feel trapped, like there is no way out! But there is! I could not have made it through this without God's help!" Sarah said. She now understands that her weight is not a reflection of her character; she was not a failure. After much professional help, her weight has stabilized. Yet she could tell you that the roller-coaster ride through an eating disorder is a nightmare.

Sarah is an intelligent, warm, and talented young woman who bought into society's perfect body lie and fell prey to an eating disorder. An estimated eight million Americans are currently afflicted with these abnormal eating patterns, with thousands losing their lives as a result each year.

True eating disorders are way beyond typical dieting. Here are a few of the most common types of eating disorders:

Anorexia Nervosa

Anorexia is addictive dieting. It is a form of self-induced starvation. Anorexics have a compulsive need for perfection and control that is usually brought on by trauma. They risk their overall health, and can suffer from loss of menstruation, irregular heartbeat, heart attack, or heart failure. Other internal organs can suffer extreme damage as well. An estimated 10 to 15 percent of anorexics die, exchanging their lives for the need to be thin.

Bulimia Nervosa

This is when a person develops intense secretive patterns of eating large quantities of food, known as binge eating. This is followed by an intense and compulsive effort to get rid of the food and the "full" feeling by some form of purging (vomiting, excessive exercise, or using laxatives or diuretics). Bulimia can lead to dangerous weight loss, kidney failure, menstrual irregularity, swollen neck glands, muscle cramps, heart complications, and internal bleeding from the tearing of the throat lining (due to excessive vomiting).

Compulsive Eating

A person who eats compulsively consumes large quantities of food, without being able to control the amount she eats. (Relax, this is more than the occasional pig-out.) The person feels compelled to eat in order to escape or numb out feelings that she is not dealing with in a healthy manner. Food alone becomes her comfort and her friend. Compulsive eaters gain unhealthy amounts of weight that can lead to obesity and health complications.

This is serious stuff! Crash diets, yo-yo dieting, and fad diets can mess up your metabolism and your menstrual cycle, and you should never abuse your body this way. Eating disorders also mess up your life.

It's true that most teens do not develop a severe, full-blown eating disorder, but thousands of you teens out there are bowing to society's pressure to be thin. An obsession with being skinny can lead to twisted thinking about food, the body, and one's personal value. This can prompt girls to "dabble" in the dangerous tactics that are commonly connected to eating disorders, such as vomiting, compulsive exercise, drastic dieting, and using diuretics or laxatives. Don't get caught in the trap. Get out of the danger zone! You are too valuable!

God has designed the body to work according to a delicate balance. Vomiting, diuretics, laxatives, compulsive exercise, and drastic dieting all mess up this balance, putting the body at risk.

How can you tell if you are in this "danger zone"? If you have concerns, it is best to talk with your doctor. However, many girls with eating disorders don't see the problem until it has created *permanent* health problems. If you—or someone you know—is caught in any of these "danger zones" it's time for you to *get help!*

To the Rescue!

Confide in your parents, a trusted adult, or your pastor. They are people who love you! They want to be your allies against an eating disorder. You can also contact one of the following organizations and ask to speak to a counselor. Don't let the problem linger. You are too valuable to just waste away! Reach out today!

Remuda Ranch
1-800-445-1900
www.remuda-ranch.com
(Christian)

Eating Disorder Awareness and Prevention (EDAP)
1-206-382-3587

www.edap.org

Girl Stuff Finale

If you ever attend one of my seminars, you'll discover I have a few trademarks. You know, things I always do, such as my infamous quizzes that are always accompanied by a candy toss. Yep. I throw candy (usually chocolate, since no event would be complete without it) to the girls who shout out the right answer.

Without a doubt, there are always girls seated way in the back who don't get their share of tasty sweets. And someone always yells, "You throw like a girl!" (thus the candyless chicks in the back).

Am I offended by their remark? No way! I just smile.

I throw like a girl because I *am* a girl! And proud of it! Being a girl, a chick, a diva, is special.

Yes, there are millions of us out there, but God made us distinctly female. As you discovered in this chapter, we are loaded with strictly "girl" hormones that cause our beautiful, one-of-a-kind bodies to blossom into full womanhood. We have a range of emotions that allow us to feel deeply and love intensely.

And we deal with some uniquely girl-related issues that very often complicate our lives (pass the tampons, please).

But now that we've chatted through a few of them, my hope is that you are standing tall, looking confident, and feeling totally jazzed about being a girl. A female. A member of a special sisterhood.

After all, God selected it for you.

He loves it when you're feeling and acting, well ... girlish! Yes, moodiness, pimples, pig-outs, and all!

So, go ahead. Celebrate your femininity.

Toss up some confetti and enjoy being a girl!

Growing Up Stuff

From Handling Parents to Priorities to Peer Pressure,
Here's Help With Some Tough Growing Up Stuff!

Collecting Keepsakes
Keep Track of Your "Growing-Up Memories" With Nancy Raney

I wish someone had clued me in about keepsakes when I was just starting out. There are so many things I saved over the years that I don't really care about now. On the other hand, I have also thought of many things I wish I *had* saved, which at the time didn't seem that important or interesting. Keepsakes are valuable because they serve as a history of your life's events and help spark some special memories. Here is a list of items to give you ideas of some things to save, some things not to save, and just some things to think about.

Awards

You know, trophies, certificates, and ribbons. You should keep them, because they're fun to think about later and one day your kids will be impressed that you were such a star, athletically or academically! I've got a scrapbook full of ribbons and awards that I have rarely been able to work into a conversation or use on a résumé, but it serves as a great reminder of things I have accomplished. What a great self-esteem booster!

Cards

If you start collecting now, can you imagine how many cards you will have by the time you are seventy? Thousands!

Here's my "save it" rule of thumb. If the person took the time to write a personal note that touched you at the time, then save it. If it was made by hand, save it. If it's a Hallmark with no personal note, toss it. Some people save cards and recycle the pictures on the front, gluing them to blank cards or turning them into postcards. You'll have to decide how crafty you are and keep them if you can turn them into an art project or a cool bulletin board for your room.

Sometimes it's fun to save birthday cards from milestones like when you turn thirteen, sixteen, twenty-one, thirty, or forty, and so on.

If you are being the kind and loving gal God wants you to be, you could end up having bunches of thank-you cards or cards of encouragement. A box full of thank-you cards can be a great testimony to your servant-like heart. Some of those notes might be just the things you need on a day you're feeling blue. So save them just for you.

Check Stubs

How about the first and last pay stub from each job you have? Someone might not believe you when you tell him or her that you made $6.25 per hour on your first job. I made $.50 an hour babysitting and $1.75 per hour at my first real job at a pizza parlor. Jobs are memories, too. Looking at a check stub can invoke all kinds of memories for you, some good, and I'm sure some bad, but all a part of who you are today.

Correspondence

Thank goodness for the age of computers! From now on when you write a letter to someone, do two things: type it on the computer and keep a copy for yourself. Letters are filled with historical information about you. If you don't have a computer, take the time to photocopy your letters before you stick them in the mail. Make a file folder for each year and just start collecting.

Notes and letters from boyfriends are OK, but when Mr. Right comes along, you might want to trash those treasures. It's not so cool to live in the past when it comes to old boyfriends.

Here's a special tip, free of charge: When you're dating that guy you think could be the one, give him a clue that he might want to save stuff from you. You know, letters, notes, gifts, and stuff. He might not be able to think of that on his own.

Journals

OK, this seems like a no-brainer, but you'd be surprised at how many people don't keep journals because they don't know what to write about. My advice? Write about everything! Your thoughts, feelings, prayers, special events, and special people! Keep a history of your life. You will appreciate being able to look back at what you've been through and what God has done in your life.

Movie and Theater Ticket Stubs

You have hundreds of movies, plays, concerts, and musicals in your future. Wouldn't it be fun to remember them all? How about saving the program, too? I guarantee they will mean even more to you if you take a minute to write a personal note to yourself about the show, who you went with, and how you felt.

Name Tags

You can't imagine how many events you will attend that will require a name tag: birthday parties, bridal showers, conventions, seminars, retreats. You get the picture? Every time you attend an event that includes a name tag, save it! When you get home, write the date and the name of the event somewhere on the name tag, or stick the name tag to a piece of paper and write on that. How about including a brief report on the event? Many memories come from "name tag" events.

Newspapers

Your life will be full of historical events, all captured on the front page of the newspaper. Save them! In my life there have been Kennedy's death, Nixon's resignation, the Vietnam War, landing on the moon, the first space shuttle, a new millennium, and most recently, the terrible tragedy of September 11. We have copies of these reports. Your kids and grand-kids will think this is cool too, when they have to write a history report and you can provide the actual newspaper.

Pictures

Of course, right? But here's a tip to start doing right now. Write the date and the event on the backs! You can't believe how much you'll forget that you swore you never would. At the very minimum, start a new box every year. That way, when you try to put them in order after you retire (like the rest of America), you might not go insane trying to remember the year they were taken.

Receipts

This might seem like an odd one, and I'm not talking about *all* your receipts. You'd have to rent a warehouse for that! I'm talking about special purchases and big firsts. For example, the first time you go grocery shopping when you move out on your own, or your first lease or rental agreement, your first appliances, or the sales slip from your first car. Or why not all your cars—there won't be hundreds of them. How about the restaurant receipt from a special night, or airline tickets? All those events that meant something to you tell the story of your life.

School Yearbooks

Last but not least, these gems will be fun to look back on forever. These are great keepsakes, but here are a few tips. When you are signing another person's book, don't try so hard to be funny, and stay away from standards like "Stay as sweet as you are," "Don't do anything I wouldn't do," or "Have a great summer!" Heartfelt notes that refer to a special event, describe your relationship, or express appreciation for someone's personal characteristics will have far more long-lasting meaningfulness.

One more tip: after people sign your book, take the time to write in their last names. After ten or twenty years go by, you might want to look up their pictures to remember who they are.

I have always felt pretty confident that I would remember everything, but I'm here to tell you one thing I know for sure. I didn't and you won't either! It is a constant amazement to me how much important stuff I can't remember that I thought I'd never forget. Collecting these keepsakes will help save the specialness of your life and keep it tucked inside your memory and your heart.

Nancy Raney is the mom of three teen girls, Kelly, Molly, and Carlly, and son Hayden. Her all-time favorite keepsake is the huge scrapbook she kept of her senior year. Nancy currently works as an administrative assistant. In her spare time she is busy making fun memories for herself and her family!

Do Whatcha Gotta Do!

Procrastination—planning to do something later, but then never doing it—can create a humongous amount of stress in a chick's life. Here's what you've gotta know: Don't put off until tomorrow what needs to be done today!

The biggest obstacle is just getting started. Try making yourself a bargain—if you work on your homework for one hour, you can take that cookie break or go for a brisk walk. Plan your rewards. But no cheating!

Once you've started, break your big tasks down into smaller ones. Then start and finish something simple. This will keep you motivated to keep going instead of sliding back into procrastination.

Challenge yourself to be decisive. Some girls put things off because they can't make a decision, but deciding not to decide *is* a decision. Seek God's direction, and then follow His lead. If you don't sense His lead, choose what you think is best and ask Him to stop you if you're headed the wrong way. The important thing is to make a decision and move ahead.

OK, now you're on a roll. Keep it up! Many well-intentioned procras-tinators have missed some great opportunities. Don't let that be you!

It is far better not to say you'll do something than to say you will and then not do it.

ECCLESIASTES 5:5

Goals 101

Do you have tons of decisions piling up and running into each other? To help you make more clear-cut decisions, you need goals. Get with God to pray over each area of your life. Then you and the Lord should set some goals.

Whether you are faced with daily decisions (like what to eat, what to wear, when to do your homework, or what to do this weekend) or future decisions (like where to go to college, what career to pursue, whom to marry, or where to settle), you can sift through your options and make decisions more effectively if you know your goals!

For example:

1. If your goal is to be a journalist, which is the better decision?
   A. Work after hours on the school newspaper.
   B. Try out for cheerleading.

2. If your goal is to save money for college, which is the better decision?
   A. Blow thirty bucks on concert tickets and pizza.
   B. Accept that baby-sitting job.

3. If your goal is to be more Christlike, which is the better decision?
   A. Get up early and go to breakfast Bible study.
   B. Sleep in.

4. If your goal is to have a better relationship with your dad, which is the better decision?
   A. Spend Saturday at the arcade.
   B. Spend Saturday mowing and weeding the yard with your dad.

5. If your goal is to be more focused, which is the better decision?
   A. Take on three new projects.
   B. Eliminate distracting activities.

6. If your goal is to build a healthier body, which is the better decision?
   A. Fast food for lunch and a sundae after school.
   B. Yogurt with fresh fruit for lunch and a bag of pretzels after school.

Check your answers: 1. A; 2. B; 3. A; 4. B; 5. B; 6. B

Get the picture? When you know your goals, decisions will be easier to make. So, here goes. Grab some paper, do some prayin', and then begin to identify your goals in each of the following areas:

Growing in Christ
Church participation
School goals
College goals
Career goals
Fitness and nutritional goals
Financial goals
Relationship goals (parents, siblings, friends)
Others

Little Hint
You'll never get there if you don't know where you are going!

Girl Power MTV Style
Calling All Girls!

A Look at the Media With Cari Stone

So, say that casting director straight off Rodeo Drive just rolled into your neighborhood in his black Mercedes Benz. He's looking for teen girls to play themselves in an upcoming MTV series. That sounds pretty cool! He's asked you to audition. That sounds even cooler! But first, he wants to find out just what kind of lady you think you're shaping up to be. So, grab a pen and mark your answers.

When it comes to being a chick, I'd like to describe myself as:
A. Sassy
B. Easygoing
C. Confident
D. Powerful

I think I look most attractive when:
A. I'm wearing an outfit that reveals just enough to keep the guys guessing
B. I'm sporting my cute workout capris and a T-shirt
C. My skin is covered, but my threads are still fashionable
D. My belly is showing

When it comes to guys, I:
A. Like to tease them—they're immature anyway
B. Am sometimes annoyed, but most of the time think they're OK
C. Think some of them are cute
D. Date a lot, but only on my terms

The coolest females are the ones who:
A. Do what they want to do, regardless of what people think
B. Remain true to their convictions
C. Are confident and glad to be female
D. Are always in charge

Someday I hope that my future contains:
A. A man, a career, and total freedom
B. A husband, a family, and a golden retriever
C. A fulfilling job and a meaningful social life
D. A life free of obligation to anyone or anything

OK. Now it's time to tally your answers. Add up all your As, Bs, Cs, and Ds.

Next, find the corresponding description so that you (and the casting director, of course) can gather some insight into where your psyche is hanging these days.

A—The Flirtatious Freedom Seeker

She often graces the screen of MTV. You'll see her in videos and shows like "Dismissed." On the one hand she seems pretty cool. She's daring, fashionable, funny, and very successful by the world's standards. There are lots of girls at school who act like her.

B—The Easygoing Relater

She is much less likely to be on the tube. You might have friends like her, or you might be her. She's down-to-earth, she's funny, and she has lots of interesting things to talk about. Not much gets her upset. She's cute—but in the more natural sense of the word.

C—The Independent Friend Finder

Not unlike the Easygoing Relater, she is more likely to show up in real life than on the movie screen. She likes adventure and isn't afraid to stand up for what she believes. Still, in those moments of conflict she tries to listen to all sides. She's the master of agreeing to disagree and seems to have lots of friends as a result.

D—The Power-Seeking Woman Warrior

Look out! This one thinks she's in charge in just about every situation. She can seem like she has a chip on her shoulder at times, although her intention rarely goes beyond simply sticking up for her own rights. She's good-looking and tough, and guys tend to fall for her. And yes, you guessed it, she, too, takes over prime-time shows more than once a week.

So, how did you make out? Are you surprised by the results? Does your personality square up with those of the stars or do you tend to blend more with the B and C ladies? Well, before you throw in the towel and consider yourself a failure by Hollywood's standards (or, on the other hand, before you pack your bags and head to the City of Angels because you, too, are a power-seeking woman warrior), read on.

Media Messages

A couple of months ago I sat down in front of the television with my notebook and green pen in hand. My mission that afternoon was to check out what MTV and the like were telling you (maybe not in so many words) about what it means to be a hip chick. It seemed my timing was perfect. When I flipped to Channel 21, there sat two teen stars, counting down the twenty hottest female videos for all of you to see. While I can't repeat the title of the show (as it contained words that would definitely be edited from a Christian book) I can tell you that over the course of the next two hours what I saw, and heard, left me feeling sad.

With each video came an introduction. One artist was esteemed for her toughness. Another for her body—most of which was in plain view. Still another was praised for her abrasive attitude and her song containing so many expletives that I lost count. One artist dressed like a demon. Another titled her song after her astrological sign. I probably don't have to tell you that this sort of thing is not limited to one channel. Neither is it limited to television. You flip through magazines, turn on the radio, or show up at the movies and all too often, this is what you're handed.

So, what's your point?

My point is simply this. Consider these thoughts a road sign. As you continue to travel life's path, let them serve as a reminder—maybe even a warning—that the messages you see on the screen, hear over the airwaves, and read in the magazines are often in conflict with who God has designed you to be. I know that these girls seem cool—as if they have it all. But don't be deceived. God's plan for you contains so much more. His power is Girl Power like you've never seen before!

Cari Stone is a freelance writer and editor who lives in Southern California with her husband, Phil. In her free time you'll likely find her jogging on the beach, swimming laps in the pool, or drinking a latte at her favorite coffeehouse.

Little Hint

**Worry does not empty tomorrow of its sorrow;
it empties today of its strength.**

Corrie ten Boom

Identity Crisis!
Discovering *You* Apart From Your Parents!
Q & A With Human Resources Consultant Caroline Reid

What is an "identity" crisis?
A "crisis" is a period of intensity, when everything seems to "come to a head." During that time, you are most likely to ask passionate questions like, "Who am I really? Do I count for anything? What's the purpose of my life? What's really important?" As we gain independence, or "separate," we develop our own opinions, our own ways of doing things. A teen's identity crisis has to do with separating from parents and knowing who she is apart from them.

When will I know I'm experiencing this?
When you want to know that it's OK to have your own opinions! When you want to have an identity separate from your parents and what they have taught you. When you know that you are special, unique.

When am I going to have an identity crisis?
Some teens are able to get through adolescence without experiencing these profound doubts and questions. For most it happens between the ages of fourteen and eighteen, although some young people don't experience it until their early twenties.

Will I have an identity crisis even if I know who I am in Christ?
If you have received Jesus into your heart and given your life to Him, then you know that you are a child of the King, you know you are precious to Him, and you know that He has a plan for your life. Even when you know who you are in Christ, you may still struggle with "separating" from your parents. Yet, knowing who Jesus is for you, and who you are to Jesus, can really help you through this separation more smoothly.

Is there anything in the Bible about identity crises?
Yes, though you won't find that exact phrase! Read the story of the Prodigal Son in Luke 15:11–32. What do you see? A young man who has to find out who he is, separate from his father. So he demands his inheritance and leaves the family farm to make his own way in the world. He explores and tries out new stuff. Ultimately he makes a lot of mistakes and comes to realize how much he appreciates his family's life. So he returns home, understanding who he is and what he needs in life.

Is my identity crisis going to be like the Prodigal Son's?
Let's hope not! You don't have to run away from home and try worldly living to discover who you are and what you believe.

Here are some of the things you may experience:

- ♥ Doubts about yourself, your parents, other authority figures, and their rules.
- ♥ Arguments with your parents, and the desire to go against their standards. (Be careful with your words and actions during this time. Remember, God tells you to honor your parents. So be respectful and make compromises when possible.)
- ♥ Experimenting with things like clothes, makeup, friends, music, language, and food to find your own likes and dislikes.
- ♥ Facing new temptations you know will "cross the line," like alcohol, drugs, sex, lying, stealing. A word of wisdom: you may feel the desire to try these things but that doesn't mean that you should do them. Each of these things (and many others, too) is dangerous and will lead you down the wrong path!
- ♥ Seeing your parents as less than perfect, seeing they have faults, too.
- ♥ Dissatisfaction, frustration, boredom, anger, and anxiety about what others think of you.
- ♥ Wanting to change the friends with whom you hang out, or clinging to close friends.
- ♥ Feeling like you want to get away from everything that is familiar.

Is there anything I can do about this crisis?
Yes. Here are some suggestions:

- ♥ Go to God! Pray, asking God to help you sort out your feelings.
- ♥ Talk about it with your close friends and you'll probably find that many of them have feelings like yours.
- ♥ Find a gal to whom you can relate, and be prayer buddies—pray with and for each other.
- ♥ Don't panic and think you are going crazy—you aren't!
- ♥ Talk with your parents about what's going on inside you. Share

your thoughts, questions, and doubts. Chances are, your mom will remember her own identity crisis! If you can't talk with your parents, find another adult woman in whom you can confide who will help you through the bad patches.

♥ Remember that you won't always feel this way. This "crisis" will come to an end.

♥ Resist the temptation to take drastic actions! Resist the temptation to do things you know are wrong! Resist temptation!

♥ Keep a journal of your feelings. You may even find a sense of release in writing poetry or songs.

♥ Choose healthy, positive outlets when you are angry, frustrated, or fearful. Try exercise, dance to praise music, call a friend who makes you laugh, or have a good cry!

How can I find help in the Bible?

Read and reread the story of the Prodigal Son. Notice what happened when he took drastic action, when he was selfish and thought only of his own needs. It caused him great unhappiness. Notice what happened when he decided to return home. His father welcomed him with love and joy. Chances are, your parents will respond the same way to you when you turn to them. Furthermore, you can depend on Jesus to meet you with love and acceptance when you turn to Him with your doubts, anger, and hurts.

Having a "lifeline verse," that gives you hope and comfort will be a continual reminder of how Jesus loves you and accepts you. Write it out, decorate the border, and tape it to your mirror, or inside your locker. Here are some possibilities:

- Romans 8:15-17
- Romans 8:38-39
- Philippians 1:6
- Philippians 4:6-7
- Psalm 139 (choose the verses that speak to you)
- Psalm 23 (this entire passage is great)

A final thought: God made you, and He is with you during this difficult period. Talk to *Him* in prayer. Ask *Him* those tough and passionate questions. He can give you patience when you feel like blowing up at someone. He can give you self-control when you need to honor your parents and appreciate your siblings. He can give you wisdom when you need to see how both good and bad family experiences are shaping you into the person He wants you to be. He can give you peace when nothing makes sense. He can even give you joy in the unfolding, developing, and separating that is part of growing up!

Caroline Reid is a former human resources consultant who currently serves as a women's ministries director in her local church. Caroline, her husband, and son Matthew live in Southern California.

Little Hint
(About Mom and Dad)

Dear Daughter,

Obey your father and your mother. Take to heart all of their advice; keep in mind everything they tell you. Every day and all night long their counsel will lead you and save you from harm; when you wake up in the morning, let their instructions guide you into a new day. For their advice is a beam of light directed into the dark corners of your mind to warn you of danger and to give you a good life. Honoring them is the same as honoring Me. You will be rewarded for doing so. I promise.

Love, Your Heavenly Father

(see Proverbs 6:20-23; Ephesians 6:1-3)

Giving Back!
Check Out Stephanie Inks' Twenty-Five Ideas to Impact Your Community

Part of growing up is recognizing that you have been blessed and now it is time to bless someone else. You can serve as God's hands and feet here on earth, and as a result, you can make a difference in your community. Go ahead, take a risk, take a step forward, take a leap of faith!

1. Serve food at a homeless shelter.
2. Collect clothes for a home for battered women.
3. Ring the bell for the Salvation Army during the Christmas season.
4. Volunteer at a crisis pregnancy center.
5. Take on an environmental project, such as planting trees.
6. Mentor a younger girl for a few hours a week through an organized program such as Big Brothers Big Sisters of America.
7. Raise funds for your favorite charity.
8. Identify needy families in your area and organize a food drive for them at Thanksgiving.
9. Start an "Angel Tree" program at your church where members donate new gifts for needy children.
10. Baby-sit for a single mother on a regular basis (for free, of course!).
11. Tutor at an elementary school.
12. Clean up and "make safe" one of your local public parks.
13. Do yard work for a shut-in.
14. Teach a child from a poor home one of your special skills, such as playing an instrument or a sport.
15. Sort books at the library.
16. Develop a weekly reading program for children.
17. Serve cookies and orange juice at a Red Cross blood drive.
18. When you are seventeen, give blood.

19. Visit a children's home.
20. Spread hope at a hospital by visiting patients or working in the gift shop.
21. Teach Sunday school or Vacation Bible School.
22. Coach at a YMCA camp.
23. Adopt a grandparent at a local nursing home and visit every week, especially on the holidays.
24. Care for animals at the local Humane Society.
25. Volunteer to do office work, such as filing, for a local charity.

Add your ideas here:

_____

_____

_____

_____

_____

_____

_____

_____

_____

_____

   Circle the ideas that you are most interested in. Now, choose one to start with. Make the needed arrangements. Take your friends along. God will bless you for reaching out to others in His name!

Stephanie C. Inks is a girl of action! She continues to "wow" many with her endless energy and giving spirit. She has labored tirelessly for the conservative community for nearly ten years through means such as community service, public speaking, writing, working in the political arena, and working in broadcast journalism.

Growing Up Spiritually

I love to read in bed at night before I go to sleep. Snuggling down into the covers with a good book relaxes me. Bill, my husband, doesn't need to "relax." When his head hits the pillow, it's snoozeville for him. He does have one requirement, however; the lights have to be *off*.

Well, it's a little hard for me to read by the light of the moonbeams shining through our mini-blinds. The answer? A little book light. Mine has a very sensitive switch; I finally get it turned on, then one tiny tap and it's off! Very moody thing. So I try to motionlessly turn the pages, oh so carefully. But to no avail. Off it goes again!

Reading in the dark is no good. I can't see the words (or the book for that matter). I can't understand the meaning. I don't get a thing out of it!

Going to church and reading the Bible can be just like that for people who don't know Jesus. The pastor's message, Sunday school class—it doesn't click with them. It's over their head, in one ear and out the other. They may attempt to read the Bible, but the yawns set in. Boring. Pointless. They have no interest in God. No desire to please Him with their lifestyle.

What's the deal? They are in darkness. The light is not on!

The Bible explains that a person who isn't a Christian cannot understand or accept the teachings and thoughts of the Spirit of God. They sound foolish to him. Why? Because only those people who know Jesus and have the Holy Spirit within them can really understand spiritual things (see 1 Corinthians 2:14).

Before a person can grow up spiritually, he or she has to be born spiritually! Listen to what Jesus told the Jewish leader Nicodemus:

> Truly, truly, I say to you, unless one is born of water and the Spirit, he cannot enter into the kingdom of God. That which is born of the flesh is flesh; and that which is born of the Spirit is spirit. Do not marvel that I said to you, "You must be born again."
>
> JOHN 3:5-7, NAS

Of course, it's not the body that gets reborn! It's the spirit. When a girl prays and asks Jesus to forgive her sins and come into her heart, God sends the Holy Spirit to live right inside her.

Jesus told the disciples:

> And I will ask the Father, and He will give you another Helper, that He may be with you forever; that is the Spirit of truth, whom the world cannot receive, because it does not behold Him or know Him, but you know Him because He abides with you, and will be in you.
>
> JOHN 14:16-17, NAS

The Holy Spirit comes to live inside of believers. One of the main jobs of the Spirit is to teach us and guide us. That's great news for discovering God's will. We have a resident teacher that is 100 percent plugged into God!

In fact, Scripture tells us that the Holy Spirit alone knows the thoughts of God. When we have received the Holy Spirit, He can reveal God's thoughts and directions to us as God wills it (see 1 Corinthians 2:10-12).

When you accept Jesus, you have already fulfilled a major portion of God's plan for your life: to be His child, part of His family. Now you've started the journey of life with the Lord. Spiritual things start to make sense. The Bible becomes your handbook to life. The lights finally come on. You can now begin to grow up spiritually!

OK, true confessions. Are you in the dark or the light? Only when you are His child will you be able to grow in Him.

Why not pray with me to be sure you are in the light, full of the Holy Spirit, and walking with the Lord?

Dear Heavenly Father,

I believe that You are God, the Creator of all things, including me. I believe that Your Son Jesus died and was raised from the dead to provide forgiveness of sin. I know I have sinned. So I ask that You, Jesus, would forgive me. I want You to come into my life to be my Lord and Savior. I open the door of my heart and let You in. Thank You for giving me eternal life. Holy Spirit, I invite you to live in me! Help me to hear the Father's voice and to grow up in Him. Guide me to do His will in my life. Keep me in the light, that I might honor and please Him in all I do.

In Jesus' name I pray, Amen.

Growing spiritually is much like growing physically. You learned to crawl, then walk, then run! It's a process. It takes time. But as you pray, read the Bible, spend time praising God, and attend church, you will deepen your walk with God and know He is the one to run to at all times. Happy growing!

God's To-Do List

The sun was setting far beyond the olive trees that filled the garden of Gethsemane. The shadows from the branches were fading as the dusk turned into night. He had separated Himself from the others. The reality of His mission was pressing in on Him. Jesus fell on His face in agony and despair.

Tears and sweat dripped from His body. His soul was "crushed with horror and sadness to the point of death." With His head in His hands, He prayed, using the last bit of breath He could force out. "My Father! If it is possible, let this cup be taken away from me. But I want your will, not mine" (Matthew 26:38-39).

What? Jesus wanted to pass on this plan? He didn't want this cup? The cup represented what He was about to do. It stood for the sins of man, which were sending Him to the cross. It stood for the cruel treatment and horrifying death He was about to experience. Who wanted to be spit on, beaten, and nailed to a cross, left for dead? Besides, He knew He would be temporarily cut off from God, His loving Father. I'll bet He was thinking, *Father, I don't know if I can do this!*

It was all too much for His human side. Part of Him didn't want to face the cross. He was scared. He was human, just like us. But He had a choice. He submitted. He surrendered His will. Jesus wanted to please His Father. He wanted the Father's will, not His own. What about you?

After you've told God how *you* want it to be, are you willing to say, "*but,* Father, I want for me what You want for me"? God's will over yours—this is tough stuff. Allowing God to set the course and call the shots takes commitment. Being sold out to God is proof you are maturing!

When you're seeking God's will, you must be willing to pray, like Jesus, "Father, Your will be done, not mine," instead of, "my will be done, not Yours."

Jesus' flesh—His human nature—wanted to say, "No way. I'm outta here." But by the power of the Holy Spirit within Him, He said yes. He went to the cross.

How can we say yes, as well? By remembering who lives in us! The Holy Spirit! When your flesh is weak and wants to say no to the things God asks you to do, rely on the Spirit to give you the strength to say yes. Then when you turn, taking steps toward God's plan, the power will be there. God will enable you to follow through.

God's will is always best. It may be harder, but it brings greater reward. Living off God's "to-do" list brings a heart full of peace, contentment, and deep joy, knowing you are doing the right thing, knowing you have said, "Thy will be done." It's part of growing up in your faith!

Little Hint
Life is not all about what you want!
It's about what God wants for you and what others want, too.

Getting Your Relationships in Order!
True Confessions of a (Not So) Super Granny Named Lynette Ward

Have you ever looked at the U.S.D.A. "Food Guide Pyramid"? It looks something like this:

Fats
Dairy & Meats
Fruits & Veggies
Hearty Grains & Cereals

You'll notice that the "foundation" or "base" of the pyramid contains the foods of which you should eat the most, with the foods at the top being those of which you should eat the least. What do you think a *relationship* pyramid would look like? How about this?

Me
Foes
Friends
Family Members
God/Jesus/Holy Spirit

As in the food pyramid, we put the most important relationship at the bottom as the foundation upon which other relationships are built. So ... who is the *least* important person in the relationship pyramid? That's right—you are! Want to guess what happens when the pyramid gets turned upside down? Yep! "Me" becomes more important than anyone else.

God/Jesus/Holy Spirit
Family Members
Friends
Foes
Me

This pyramid doesn't look too stable, does it? It can get knocked over pretty easily, or even topple on its own. Why? Because it's focused on "self," which almost always leads to selfishness!

Here comes the confession part. Let me backtrack just a little. I love being a "granny" better than any other "job" of my life, and have wonderful relationships with all of my grandchildren. I've worked at it a bit, putting their pleasure and needs ahead of my own. (I recently attended a DC Talk concert with the eleven-year-old and had a blast, but my ears haven't forgiven me yet!) The family has frequently called me "Super Granny." Well, guess what ... "Super Granny" messes up, just like everyone else.

Here's the story, from my perspective. My oldest granddaughter, who was the magical age of thirteen when this occurred, has always been bonded to me in a special way. She has wanted me to be a part of everything in her life, until ... she suddenly perceived me as being a liability in her goal of getting backstage to meet her fave boy band, Plus One. To be honest, I probably *was* a liability in this situation, but the way it played out wasn't pretty. We had talked about going to a festival where the guys were going to sing, and I was really looking forward to it. I won't go into all the gory details, but when I began to sense that something was wrong and that I wasn't wanted, I was crushed. I, the one who had always enjoyed kids and anything connected with them, suddenly felt old and unwanted for the first time in my life.

Did I, the "mature" one, put myself at the bottom or the top of the relationship pyramid? You guessed it. I dug in my heels, focused on *my* pain and *her* selfishness, and forced her to tell me point-blank that she didn't want me to go. (At least she loved me enough that she didn't *really* want to say it.) The big problem here is that we *both* had ourselves and our desires at the bottom of the pyramid. We were balancing our pyramids on ourselves, and it brought great grief to us both. Did we get those pyramids turned right side up? Yes, thanks to Jesus and His love for us and His forgiveness, we did, but it took several months of really uncomfortable interaction.

There is always a price to pay for sin, and selfishness is *always* sin. It's not right for us Christian women, young or old, to put ourselves, and what we want, ahead of others. The Bible even says so!

Do nothing from selfishness or empty conceit, but with humility of mind let each of you regard one another as more important than himself; do not merely look out for your own personal interests, but also for the interests of others.

PHILIPPIANS 2:3-4, NAS

Does that mean that we don't matter? Of course not! But it does mean that we are not to think of ourselves first!

So, remember that other people have feelings (even grown-ups and grannys) and that you will do well to keep your relationship pyramid in the proper order.

Lynette Ward gets the "Grandmother of the Decade" award! But she is not only a good granny, she's also a wonderful friend. Besides being with grandchildren, she enjoys teaching the youth at her church and taking trips to the beach. Lynette and her husband Barry live in Covington, Louisiana.

Little Hint

Society has given us women the "right" to be totally selfish and self-absorbed for one particular event of our lives—our weddings. "The bride should have whatever she wants!" No matter what anyone else needs or wants and no matter who gets hurt or how badly? No way! Surprise everyone, girls, and make your wedding a time of peace, joy, and reverence. Let your love for your groom (and your family and friends) be expressed in your kind, patient, and unselfish actions! Be a bride who is beautiful inside and out!

The Patience Thing

Traffic signals are great. They keep the flow of cars going in an orderly fashion. Without them, there would be total confusion, tons of fender benders, and more crashes!

God's Word, like a traffic signal, gives us direction. Sometimes when we pray about which road to follow, we get a green light: GO. Other times it's red: STOP. Very often we get a yellow: WAIT. Stop and go are pretty easy to understand. But yellow, that's a tricky one.

Does God want you to proceed with caution or prepare to stop?

Maybe He wants you to stay where you are and patiently wait for His timing or His clear direction.

Waiting on the Lord is more than being stuck somewhere between stop and go. It's not the land of limbo! It's not time to kick back and get comfy. Waiting on the Lord is not a time to do nothing. It's not passive; it's active!

Here are some *active* steps for you to take while you wait for God to clear your path, give you direction, or answer your prayers.

Pray. Bring your requests or situation before the Lord every day. Pursue an answer with diligence. Ask God to show you His purpose, His timing, and His way of doing things. "Ask,... seek,... knock" (Matthew 7:7-8, NAS).

Read. Start with the Bible. Get into God's presence and find out what the Word says about your situation. Observe how God worked in the lives of Bible characters. Read Christian books that relate to whatever you are waiting for. "God's Word is a light to your path" (see Psalm 119:105).

Watch. Expect God to do something. Maybe He needs to rearrange your circumstances or change your attitude before He can move you ahead. "Eagerly watch and wait expectantly" (see Psalm 5:3).

Be patient. Don't be impulsive; don't run ahead of God! Resist the desire to devise a backup plan in case God doesn't come through—He will! No grumbling or complaining. Trust Him. He knows what He's doing. "Receive God's promises through faith and patience" (see Hebrews 6:12).

Don't quit. Use waiting periods to grow closer to God. Let His divine power recharge your battery. He will keep you keepin' on. "God renews your strength when you wait" (see Isaiah 40:31).

Seek wise counsel. Get wisdom from older, mature Christians. Select those you trust and respect. Their experience with God will give you insight while you wait. "Seek counsel and have victory" (see Proverbs 11:14).

Listen. Don't turn down the sound just because you're in God's waiting room. Now's the time to tune in. God is faithful. He will eventually speak to you. Keep doing the last thing He told you to do until He gives you something new. "Speak, Lord, for your servant is listening" (see 1 Samuel 3:9).

Little Hint

Too many expectations can leave you feeling disappointed, maybe even frustrated, that things didn't work out the way you thought they would. Why not replace those fickle expectations with faith-filled flexibility?

A flexible attitude will make your ride through life less bumpy. A flex-ible attitude will keep you calm. It will increase your patience, which is a mark of maturity! You'll be more content knowing God is in control. Flexibility helps you go with the flow. It's a pathway to peace. Plus, flexible people don't get bent out of shape!

Using Is Losing

The Monday morning buzz.

"Oh, my gosh, I had the biggest hangover this weekend—you would not believe!"

"You won't guess what happened to Mandy. She was so wasted she ended up with this guy in the back of somebody's car. She didn't even know who he was."

"Did you hear that Kevin downed a fifth and smoked pot Friday night? The guys left him at the park and someone saw him and called 911. The hospital called his parents. He's *so* in trouble."

Beer, wine coolers, hard liquor, pot, ecstasy, cocaine, heroin. Every teen alive, including you, will be faced with alcohol and drugs at some point, whether it's in junior high, high school, or college. It's illegal. It's dangerous. It's not part of God's best for us. It never, ever leads to anything good. Listen to some wise words from Proverbs:

> *Whose heart is filled with anguish and sorrow? Who is always fighting and quarreling? Who is the man with bloodshot eyes and many wounds? It is the one who spends long hours in the taverns, trying out new mixtures. Don't let the sparkle and the smooth taste of strong wine deceive you. For in the end it bites like a poisonous serpent; it stings like an adder. You will see hallucinations and have delirium tremens, and you will say foolish, silly things that would embarrass you no end when sober.*

PROVERBS 23:29-33

> *Wine gives false courage; hard liquor leads to brawls; what fools men are to let it master them, making them reel drunkenly down the street!*

PROVERBS 20:1

Drugs and alcohol are a losing game. Yet teens still drink and use drugs. Why? For lots of different reasons. Maybe they want to numb out, escape, or lessen the pain. Some use them to help them lighten up or party hearty, thinking it's a blast. Others want to fit in, be part of the group. They may feel pressure from peers to take a puff or pop a pill. Then there are those who are angry inside and use alcohol and drugs to blow off steam. Yet they don't solve a person's problems. They usually make them worse.

What about Christian teens? Research shows that kids in the kingdom are gulping down the "brewskis," too. I have seen lots of youth group kids fall into the drinking trap. What's up with that?

I believe it's because they are forgetting who they are. They are children of God Himself, transferred out of Satan's kingdom into God's! They are seated in heavenly places with Christ, able to come into God's presence with confidence. They are greatly loved by a heavenly Father who was willing to give His only Son's life to buy them back and provide forgiveness for their sin, a Father who will help them through every tough time. They are chosen, holy, set apart for God's purposes. They are royalty, made to be kings and priests before the Lord (see Revelation 1:6).

Proverbs 31:4 states that it is not for kings to drink wine or for rulers to desire strong drink. Romans 13:13-14 instructs, "Don't spend your time in wild parties and getting drunk.... But ask the Lord Jesus Christ to help you live as you should, and don't make plans to enjoy evil."

When that beer or joint is passed your way, will you let peer pressure push you around? Will you forget who you are in Christ, or remember that you are a child of an awesome God? The choice is yours. Choose wisely.

And do not get drunk with wine, for that is dissipation, but be filled with the Spirit.

EPHESIANS 5:18, NAS

Little Hint

Being a Christian yet living in an ungodly way creates inner conflict. One foot in the kingdom of God and one foot in the world doesn't work. They don't mix. You can't blend them. Swing both feet over the fence and plant both in God's kingdom. You will have peace in your life only when you are single-mindedly set on God!

Job Jitters
Here's the Inside Edition With Caroline Reid

Interviewing for a job—at some point every girl has to face this one. Chances are, you'll have many interviews for different jobs over your working lifetime. Each one will make you nervous, but each one will teach you something. In addition to looking for specific job skills or abilities depending on the job, all bosses look for more or less the same things when hiring. So here's some important information to help ease the tension and land you the job you want!

Interview Preparation: Check Out This Checklist

Gather some facts. What type of job are you looking for? What type of work would best fit your personality? What hours are you available? What are the requirements of the job in which you are interested? These may be listed in the job advertisement, or you can call and ask. Be realistic. If you meet the requirements, go for it. If not, look for something that is a better match for you.

Call to make an appointment for your interview. Get the following information:

✓ Time, date, and place of interview
✓ Name of the person who will conduct the interview, and his or her title
✓ What information you'll need to bring with you (e.g., résumé, work permission from your parents or school, current transcript, letters of recommendation)

Make that all-important choice about what to wear. Seriously, this is important. The first impression you make walking through the door will last a long time and may determine if you are hired or not! You are not dressing for a prom, nor are you going to hang out with your friends. If you are not sure what to wear, ask your mother or an aunt and follow her advice. Avoid the following: too much makeup, chipped nail polish, elaborate hairdos, lots of jewelry, bare midriffs, short skirts, tight pants or sweaters, super high heels, or low-cut tops.

It's always best to be conservative—even if you are applying for a job in a cool clothing store. The idea is to look professional, well-groomed, and put-together!

Make a list of potential questions. Based on the type of job for which you are applying, do some brainstorming and think through the kinds of questions you might be asked during the interview. Help from an adult might be good!

Prepare your answers to these questions. Nothing fancy, just think about how you'd answer questions like: "Why do you want to work here? Have you had any experience in this type of position? What is your greatest strength?"

Prepare questions about the job. Remember that this interview is a two-way process—a chance for them to decide if they want *you* and also for *you* to decide if you want them! Ask about the job. Some suggestions:

- What are the duties of this job? (You may not even have to ask this.)
- What is the most important aspect of this job? (This will help you understand the boss' philosophy and how your performance will be judged.)
- What is the most challenging part of this job? (You may have already figured this out, but it will be interesting to see what the boss says!)

- What is the work schedule? How far in advance is the schedule posted? Is there flexibility in case I have a conflict with another activity? (Don't ask this question first—it gives the wrong impression.)
- Is there a uniform or a dress code? (Looking around at other employees will give you a good idea of how to dress for work.)

Prepare yourself for the outcome. There is one more component to your job preparation: prayer! Pray over your preparation. Pray before you go into the interview and pray after you finish. Ask friends and family to pray for you. Above all, pray for God's will to be done. If you don't get the job, you can be assured that God had a reason for it, and you can trust Him to bring a better opportunity along soon.

All of these items so far have had to do with preparing yourself. If you think this is too much trouble to go to, ask yourself how important this job is to you.

The next checklist relates to the interview itself. Because you can't really carry this list into the interview with you, read and think about these items beforehand!

Interview Checklist: Now It's Time for the Real Deal

- ☐ Be on time, be on time, be on time, and finally, be on time. If necessary be early, so you can be on time!
- ☐ When you greet anyone—whether it's the boss or the receptionist—smile and make eye contact. This makes you appear friendly and confident. The boss will ask others who meet you what their impressions are. Make a good one!
- ☐ Introduce yourself and state your name clearly. (Absolutely no candy, gum, or tongue rings!)
- ☐ When asked to sit down, sit straight but comfortably, crossing your legs at the ankle.

☐ Listen carefully to all questions, while making good eye contact. No matter how nervous you may be, no matter how dry your mouth or tied your tongue may be, speak clearly. It's not a matter of volume or accent. It's a matter of pronouncing words clearly and not mumbling. Slow down, if needed. This is something you can practice beforehand with a friend or a parent, or in front of a mirror. Now, don't giggle—practicing for an interview is a good idea!

☐ If you don't know something, say so.

☐ If needed, take the time to think about your answer.

☐ If you don't understand the question, ask for clarification.

☐ Be honest and truthful. The world is full of stories about those who have lied in an interview and later had it come back to haunt them. So ... don't say you love working with people if you hate it!

☐ If asked about some skill or experience you don't have, admit you don't have it, but offer instead what you *do* have and what you *have* done that might be related. For example: "I haven't done office work before, but I am really organized with my school schedule and assignments and I help my dad with filing for his business." Or perhaps: "I haven't worked in a store before, but I help out on our church's Sunday morning coffee cart, selling coffee and cookies and operating the cash box."

☐ Ask the questions you have prepared. If the boss doesn't ask if you have questions, then introduce your questions with something like this: "Excuse me, before we finish, may I ask some questions?" Be sure to say thank you for the answers you get. The answers and the way the boss speaks to you will give you a good feeling for whether you really want to work here!

Although many of the specifics will change according to what sort of job you are applying for, this checklist will be applicable to almost any interview. Happy job hunting!

Whatever you do, do your work heartily, as for the Lord rather than for men.... It is the Lord Christ whom you serve.

COLOSSIANS 3:23-24, NAS

Caroline Reid developed this checklist after years of interviewing for jobs, from retail sales to corporate management. She has interviewed many candidates as well. She knows her stuff!

Little Hint

There are many ways to earn money—baby-sitting, a paper route, flipping burgers, waitressing—but the key is what you do with that money! Remember that God owns it, He lends it to you to manage responsibly, and He expects you to tithe (give 10 percent of it back to Him). When you do this, He will bless you (and trust you) with more!

M.I.A. Moms and Dads

I love taking our youth group girls away for the weekend. We pile into the vans—sleeping bags, pillows, and backpacks in tow—armed with tons of popcorn, hot chocolate, donuts, CDs—all the things you need for a successful sleepover!

One thing we always do is break up into small groups and pray for each other. One Friday night, in my group, we listened as Tiffany talked about her home life. The focus shifted from her mom to her dad. Well, what dad? That was the problem. Tiffany was fifteen years old and she had never met her dad. She knew he lived somewhere in the same state, but he had never contacted her. As she shared how that made her feel,

I noticed that Kim looked down as she wiped away her falling tears.

When Tiffany was finished sharing, I asked Kim if she was willing to tell us what was making her cry.

"I just feel so bad for Tiff. She's a really neat girl and her dad is missing out. And she is missing out, too. My dad is the most important person in my life. He helps me with chemistry and tries to come to all of my soccer games. I can always hear him cheering me on—OK, sometimes it embarrasses me, but it means everything to me to know he's there. I just wish Tiffany could know what that's like."

Reaching across our circle of friends, Tiffany and Kim hugged hard and cried softly. Then we joined hands and prayed for Tiffany.

Do you hurt because of a "missing" parent? Maybe it's your dad, maybe it's your mom. Maybe there's been a divorce, maybe a death. Maybe your parents are there physically but not emotionally. Maybe you feel rejected, ignored, or overly criticized. Can I pray with you, just like we prayed for Tiffany? Here, reach out and take my hand.

Heavenly Father,
We thank You that Your Word promises You are a Father to the fatherless and that You know how to comfort us like a mother. Help us to focus on You, to give You our pain and our disappointments, and to remember that You are able to be all that we need.

We love You.
In Jesus' name, Amen.

Little Hint
Part of growing up is learning to rely on the Lord.
Get your approval, attention, and affection from Him!

Growing Up Stuff Finale

You are making memories. Right here, right now, whatever you choose to do or not do in your life is creating an experience. An event. Something for today. But tomorrow it becomes a memory. It becomes something you look back on.

♥ Are you creating good memories during these "growing-up" years?

♥ Are you collecting an album full of Kodak moments to keep in the treasure chest of your heart?

♥ Are you making informed decisions, setting goals, getting your priorities in line with God's Word?

♥ Are you practicing patience in your relationships with God and with your parents?

♥ Are you using prayer as a means of discovering who you are and who God has created you to be?

Or have the alluring messages from the media or the influence of peers led you onto a path that won't be worth remembering?

This is not a very comforting thought, but it's true. Here it is.

You only get *one shot* at your teen years.

Though many girls try to blame most of the bummers of life on others, usually they have no one to point a finger at except themselves (OK, yes, there are things that are out of your control, but you know what I'm talking about).

It all comes down to choices. Every day is full of them.

Be aware. Pay attention. They are shaping you. They are the key in determining whether your memories will end up in your mental save or delete file.

Fill these "growing-up" years with memories worth keeping. Make some great choices. You'll be glad you did!

Girlfriend Stuff

From Making New Friends to Keeping Old Ones,
Here's Some Stuff on the Secrets to Tight Friendships!

Recipe for Keeping Your Friendships Sweet

Gather the following ingredients and prepare to mix them together with an attitude of openness and caring:

- Loyalty—stand by her side 24/7!
- Trust—strive to be dependable!
- Forgiveness—let things go and forget them!
- Genuineness—be real; there's no need to impress!
- Equality—don't treat her like she's more or less valuable than you!
- Goofiness—be silly; it's part of the kid in you!
- Creativity—avoid getting stuck in a rut; do fun stuff!
- Confidentiality—always keep her secrets!
- Openness—share your secrets, your dreams, your clothes!
- Encouragement—use your words to boost her self-esteem. Be her personal cheerleader!

Heap all ingredients together. No need to measure the amount—measuring up never pays off. Now blend with love at high speed. Pour into a big, heart-shaped pan and bake for a lifetime.

Freshman Freak
Feeling Left Out? Knowing God Cares Really Counts!
Just Ask Barbra Minar

I sat on the back step in the hot September sun, looking through the Friday mail. No invitation to Caroline Miller's back-to-school party. Nothing but junk mail and stuff for my folks. I'd kept hoping the invitation was lost or something. Today's mail was my last chance. The party was Saturday night. I looked again. Nope, it wasn't there. I just wanted to vanish from the earth.

"Phone for you, honey," said my mom through the screen door. "It's Cindy."

"Tell her I'll call back," I said. I just couldn't tell Cindy I wasn't invited to Caroline's party. Of course she would be going. Popular, petite little Cindy with her big brown eyes, long lashes, and tiny waist. The girl every boy goggled at and every girl wanted as her best friend. I couldn't stand the idea of starting high school. At 5'10" I would probably be the tallest, freakiest freshman girl in the history of Gulfport High School. And my feet! Size ten and a half. My shoes looked like boats. I was so skinny I had to wave my arms for anyone to see me. I was so flat-chested I didn't even need a bra. I was so nearsighted I had to put glasses on just to brush my teeth. To make matters worse, I'd gotten this bright idea to cut my long thick hair short. What a horrible mistake. Frantically I had washed it, curled it, stretched it, gelled it. Nothing helped. I looked like a freak. No wonder I wasn't invited to the party. If I had a party, I probably wouldn't invite me, either.

My grandma's stinging words haunted me. "Barbra Kay, you're growing like a weed." She was right. God had grown me into a weed. How could He possibly love me? He didn't even care how I felt!

Finally I stood up on my long grasshopper legs and went inside with the mail to help my mom around the house. While I folded the laundry and put away the clean dishes, my mind whipped like a double-Dutch jump rope. *I'm not invited. I'm a skinny, stupid, four-eyed, flat-chested freak!* I rubbed away the tears leaking down my cheeks.

At 3:00 P.M. I went across the street to baby-sit. Five-year-old Lisa sat on the couch with her arms crossed, little chin on her chest. Her mother hurried out the door, late for an appointment, saying that Lisa wasn't in a good mood. For over an hour Lisa wouldn't look at me. She didn't even smile when I told her knock-knock jokes and sang *"John Jacob Jingleheimer Smit."*

"What's the matter, Lisa?"

Finally she blurted out, "My kitten Pumpkin died." I opened my arms. She climbed into my lap and sobbed. We spent the rest of the afternoon talking about Pumpkin, making a cross, and gathering zinnias and petunias for his little grave under the pine tree.

"Does God love Pumpkin?" Lisa asked, looking down at the fresh dirt mound where her dad had buried the cat.

"God loves everything He creates. Especially you, sweetie. He knows how you feel and He cares when you are sad."

"God loves you, too," said Lisa. "And I love you." She squeezed my long legs until we toppled over. She began to laugh.

After dinner that night, I daydreamed about the party and all the fun I would miss. I peered through my glasses into the mirror at my short hair and tried to tug the bangs a little longer. It still looked horrible. Looking closer, I could see two new zits forming on my nose. What other hideous thing could happen before school started? Maybe I would grow nine more inches before Monday. I wanted to sob like Lisa. *God, don't You care what's happening? I'm ugly and left out of everything.*

The phone rang.

"Hey, Barbra Kay," said Cindy. "I was just wondering. Well, if you're not busy tomorrow night maybe we could catch a movie. Maybe you could even spend the night if you want."

I could hardly believe what she had said. Cindy, the cutest girl in our class. "Aren't you going to Caroline's party?"

"Well, no. But you're probably going. Sorry I called." Cindy sounded sort of choked up.

"No. No, I'm not going. A movie would be great. Spending the night too," I said. "Maybe you could help me with the mess I made of my hair."

As we made our plans, my heart lifted. And I remembered what I'd told Lisa. *God knows how you feel. And He cares when you are sad.* If God was with me, maybe I could live with being tall. Maybe He knew how I felt about my zits and my hair and my skinny, skinny body. Maybe I wasn't such a freak to Him. Maybe high school was going to be OK.

I smiled from the inside out.

Barbra Minar is an author, wife, mother, and grandmother. She is also a skilled listener who has had many heart-to-heart chats with friends. Her books include Unrealistic Expectations, Close Connection, Lamper's Meadow, *and* Walking Into the Wind: Being Healthy With a Chronic Disease. *Barbra and her husband Gary live in Solvang, California.*

Buddy Busters

Are you wrecking your friendships? Why be one of those girls who never realizes what she has done to ruin a good relationship? Here are some insights into the attitudes and actions that can take a friendship to the edge (or the end, if you're not paying attention)! Behaving in these ways will cause others to push away. Beware! Be wise! Don't wreck it! Don't do these things:

☹ Be closed. Never sharing what's going on in that pretty little head and heart of yours keeps friends at a distance and feeling left out. Open up!

☹ Make paybacks. Revenge is an ugly thing. Getting even for something your friend did to you will never have positive results. Forgive her and let God take care of the rest (see Romans 12:9-21).

☹ Interrupt her. If you continually break in when your friend is sharing a story or giving you a play-by-play of the big blowup she had with her parents, you'll communicate that you don't really care. Interrupting is rude. Be patient.

☹ Take her for granted. Using your friend or making her feel unappreciated always puts a crimp in a friendship. Let her know you value her.

☹ Leak a secret. Breaking a confidence is a huge offense. Don't be found guilty! Be a safe place for her. Zip your lip!

☹ Point out her imperfections. No one likes someone else to constantly remind them of their shortcomings. When you are critical it makes others feel like they aren't good enough for you. Choose to be accepting and kind.

☹ Put yourself first. Being selfish is sure to set the friendship brakes in motion. Be considerate of your friend and her needs and desires, too.

☹ Try to outdo her. Whether you're aware you are doing it or not, competing with your friend is a no-no! Wanting to one-up her will drive her away. So will trying to steal her attention (especially around guys). Be her encourager, her biggest fan!

☹ Borrow all her money. Sharing and paying back is one thing, but mooching is another. If you borrow a few bucks, always pay it back.

☹ Never tell the truth. Lying and being dishonest is a friendship squelcher for sure! In some cases, you have to tell the truth (always in love) in order to keep the relationship healthy. If you bottle up anger against your friend, you may eventually lash out. Be honest with her.

☹ Crush on the same guy. This is huge. Many good friendships have taken a nosedive over this one. You'll be wise to never like the same guy, and especially not at the same time.

☹ Smother her. Wanting to keep your friend all to yourself might backfire. Everyone needs different kinds of friends, so don't be jealous of her *other* gal pals!

☹ Be hot and cold. Playing Jekyll and Hyde is hazardous to your healthy friendship. If you're loving and then hateful, you'll leave your friend confused, not knowing where she stands with you. So be consistent. Even on a PMS day, let her know it's not her that's causing your moodiness.

Little Hint

Choose friends who are on the same road you are on— the godly one! Surround yourself with those who will influence you for good, who will pray for you, who will be a support. Being tight with girls who don't love God can cause you to take your eyes off of Him. You may find yourself beginning to doubt, disregard, and dishonor God and His Word. Yes, you need to befriend nonbelievers in order to lead them to the Lord. But be wise. If they start leading you, you'll be headed in the wrong direction.

Do not be deceived: "Bad company corrupts good morals."

1 CORINTHIANS 15:33, NAS

The Conversation Connection:
Make Some New Friends With Tonya Ruiz and Nancy Anderson's Helpful Hints

Penny took on a big project in 1972 when she began giving private English lessons to a one-year-old. Her student now understands two thousand words, initiates conversations, and knows sign language. That's amazing, considering the fact that her student, Koko, is a lowland gorilla.

What's even more astounding is the fact that God has given us—humans—so many words to learn and use. Did you know there are almost 820,000 words in the English language? That's a lot of words to choose from! So why is it sometimes so hard to find the right words to say when you meet someone? (Remember, you have an advantage here because you're not a furry, banana-breathing gorilla!)

The dictionary says that conversation is talking together or informal talk that takes place between two or more people. Having a conversation is like passing an invisible ball back and forth, with each person taking a turn (exchanging information). So what you really need to know is how to be a good talker. How hard can that be? What do you mean you're not good at talking? If you want to be good at something, you have to work at it. You can't pick up a tennis racket, take up diving, or begin figure skating and expect to win an Olympic gold medal right away. It requires skill and practice.

Have you ever told a joke, given an oral report, acted out a scary story at a slumber party, or made a new friend? Then you're well on your way to being a talker.

Let's begin. Imagine you're sitting in the cafeteria and someone you don't know sits next to you at the lunch table—the first step is to be friendly. The Bible says that to have friends you must be friendly. A smile doesn't cost you anything and instantly puts those around you at ease. Be relaxed, warm, and yourself.

Extend your hand and introduce yourself. Don't sit back with your arms crossed—open up, lean forward, and make eye contact. "Hello, my name is Stephanie Morris ... and you're?" or "Hi, I'm Stephanie Morris.... What's your name?"

Repeat the person's name after the introduction: "Hello, Veronica, it's nice to meet you!" Using a person's name makes him or her feel special and helps you remember it the next time you see that person!

What do you say after you say "Hello"? Find a conversation starter. Have you ever watched a talk show and noticed how the host gets the people to open up and talk about themselves? Oprah has an advantage because she already knows something about the people that she is about to interview, but with a little detective work, you can, too. Look for clues and ask questions.

Example:

Notice Veronica's clothes. "So, Veronica, is blue your favorite color?"

"Yes, blue is my favorite color. What's yours?" She might ask.

Listen for an accent. "Are you from around here?"

"I just moved here and I don't know anyone," she might reveal.

Is she reading a book? "I love mysteries, too," you could tell her.

"I just started this book—have you read it?" she might want to know.

Try to ask open-ended questions—those that can't be answered with a one-word answer.

Example: "How is this school different from your old one?" or "What was your favorite part of that movie?" or "What do you think about the new history teacher?"

A sincere compliment is always a good conversation starter. People will respond.

Example: "I really like the way you presented your topic on the debate team. How did you do your research?"

At this point, the "ball" is rolling and you can cover any topic that comes to mind—school, sports, music, clothes, the weather, or even boys! The key to conversation is discovering information about the other person, revealing facts about yourself, and being a good listener.

With words, we can share our hopes, dreams, fears, and secrets. Words can provide comfort, inspiration, and encouragement. Being a good conversationalist is a skill that will be an asset to you throughout your life: in school, in the workplace, in your family, and in your church. And the best part of all is that it can result in some really special, life-long friendships.

Tonya Ruiz and Nancy Anderson are two creative ladies who have mastered the art of conversation. They even write plays together! Tonya, a former professional model, has written a new book, Beauty Quest. *Tonya and Nancy live with their families in Southern California.*

Little Hint

Jesus had twelve friends with whom He spent His time. Of the twelve, three of them became His closest friends. Yet, there were times He felt lonely. It's normal to experience loneliness, but take a tip from Jesus. Always remember that even in your loneliness you are never alone. Your heavenly Father is always—yes, always—with you!

Yet I am not alone, because the Father is with Me.
JOHN 16:32, NAS

Sister, Sister:
Finding a Friend in the Family With Brio Girl 2002, Katie Pretzel

I love being with my girlfriends. We like to talk late into the night, and we can die laughing at the silliest things. Of course, we also like to shop, bake, watch movies, go out to eat, travel around town, work out, take pictures, and naturally, there's nothing like a good cry! When we do things together it feels like I am always learning something new about them. It's awesome and exciting. There is continually something to discover about your friends.

But then again, it's even *more* exciting when you already know someone—inside and out, through and through—and you continue to be best friends! It's amazing!

That's the feeling I have with my sister.

Having lived with her in the same house for nearly seventeen years, we basically know *everything* there is to know about each other (OK, not everything—that would be impossible). I know when she's going to laugh at something, or be upset. I know what she's going to say before she says anything. I know whom she's going to like and who won't make it onto her favorite person list. I know what her heart is saying. Because we have been open and talked so much, I know her dreams, goals, and aspirations. It's fun to know someone just about as well as you know yourself!

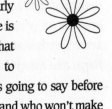

Yes, we have totally annoyed each other at times, but have chosen to work through our differences and to forgive each other when needed. We have been through good times and bad times, but we have done it together.

I am so thankful for all my sister has done and continues to do for me. She has taught me about life, about what to do and what not to do in high school. She's showed me how to make good choices about how to spend my time and with whom. She has helped me know how to deal with things like rules, parents, school, and scholarship forms! She has been my role model, my guide, and my inspiration. I could never thank her enough for being there for me. She is amazing. She is the perfect BSF—that's Best Sister Forever!

I truly believe that the main reason we have been so successful at having a close friendship is Christ. He has definitely made a difference in our relationship. His character clearly shone through my sister as she never, ever gave up on me when I was going through a huge struggle in eighth grade. She never thought less of me, but continued to love and care for me. (And to pray for me!)

Now that I've bragged about my sister, let me ask: How is your relationship with your sister (or brother)? Do you feel the same way about your sibling as I do about mine? Do you share your thoughts and dreams? Do you forgive when things get rough? If so, that's awesome! I encourage you to continue to nourish that relationship! You will be thankful that you put time into this friendship.

If you are not close with your siblings, starting today, try to develop a better friendship. There might be some arguments or misunderstandings that need to be resolved. Do it. There might be some feelings that need to be brought out into the open and dealt with. Do it. There might be some forgiveness that needs to be offered—even if something wasn't your fault. Do it. You can create a special bond between the two of you that can never be broken. It all starts with your effort to create that bond. Please don't wait another day to start building up your friendship with your sister (or brother).

Katie Pretzel is the 2002 BRIO Girl! She is a high school senior from Plymouth, Minnesota, who loves pottery, Rollerblading, and receiving mail. But her favorite thing of all is when her sister comes home from college for the weekend!

Little Hint

Make every day "Sibling Appreciation Day." Write your sister or brother a card, take him or her out to lunch, go to a movie, or hit the mall for some shopping. Or just take a long walk and talk about everything that's going on in your lives. Then, be brave and pray for each other. It's worth it.

Giving Up the Grudge:
Great Advice From This "Secret" Big Sis

What a warm, cozy feeling I used to get, thinking that my girlfriends would always be part of my life. You too? Probably right now you are gathering up school day memories, and soon the best one of all will occur: Graduation! Then there will be college, and yes, falling in love and getting married. Together with your girlfriends you have probably already spent hours dreaming about your weddings. Some of your friendships will be long lasting. Yet they won't be, unless you have a very key quality: letting go of a grudge!

As I look back over my relationships with my lifelong friends Susan, Becki, and Abbie, I can pinpoint specific times with each of them where we had to forgive one another or else the friendship would have ended.

Susan lied to me about sneaking my fluffy white sweater out of my closet. She claimed I lent it to her, but I didn't, and she was definitely wearing it. After college, Becki became too busy to even return my calls, sending the message that frantically climbing the corporate ladder was more important than our friendship. When I suspected my high school heartthrob was cheating on me, Abbie was there to console me. Then I caught them together. *She* was the "other woman." That was a tough one! Yet, if I had not forgiven her, I would have missed out on having the greatest maid of honor.

Grudges ruin everything. They're like dams that stop the free-flowing river of love and acceptance between friends. If the dam remains closed, the water level backs up and rises. Likewise, our resentment and bitterness levels will rise as long as we hang tight to past grudges and refuse to forgive.

To be honest, I have struggled with holding grudges, because it can feel as if by forgiving I am saying that what the person did to me was all right! And that's not true.

It is not OK that they lied, stole, betrayed me, or purposely hurt me.

Forgiving does not make their actions OK, but it does release the lever on the dam and allow the river of love to start trickling again, with the hopes of getting it back to flowing freely—full of love—once again. And that feels much better than the yucky feelings in the pit of my stomach when I refuse to let go of the grudge and get over it.

I have learned that I need to take my friend to the Lord. I can acknowledge my feelings, but then I need to lay them at Jesus' feet and leave them there. He ever so gently reminds me, amidst my tears or my rage, that He has forgiven me for my wrongdoings and I, in turn, must forgive others.

Then as I choose to do that, He fills me with the strength and mercy I need to mend the friendship and keep going. I know it is hard to understand why our friends do what they do, but believe me, letting go of the grudge is the only way to maintain a relationship with those friends you want to keep in your life for a long, long time!

And be kind to one another, tender-hearted, forgiving each other, just as God in Christ also has forgiven you.

EPHESIANS 4:32, NAS

Girlfriend to Girlfriend:

Check Out These Lessons From High School With BRIO Girl 2001, Kristie Kleinow

It is my senior year of high school, and I love it. I'm not saying life is perfect, but God is just sooo good. There aren't even enough "o's" in the world to stick on the end of "sooo" to express how much His grace amazes me. I look at my high school years, and I see how God has grown me up and gifted me, and how He has held my hand through it all. It has been the challenges—the loneliness at school, the friends and people who have let me down, the hurtful relationships, the breakups with boyfriends, the failures, the standing up for Christ at my public school, and the list goes on—that I've battled thus far that have been vital to the joy I now have. And I rejoice because I know that as I walk the roads of the rest of my life, I will face endless new struggles at every twist and turn, but as a daughter of the Most High King, His Word promises in 2 Corinthians 9:8 that "God is able to make all grace abound to you, that always having all sufficiency in everything, you may have an abundance for every good deed" (NAS). Wow—with a promise like that, I can't help but fall in love with the Lord and rest in His peace.

As I meet and hang out with younger girls, I find myself eager to share with them the lessons God has taught me so far. I'm not full of wisdom yet, but my young eyes are capable of seeing the marvelous things God has done, and my heart is more than ready to share with you the top four lessons He has taught me! They just might meet you where you are.

God Makes Things Work Out

In the earlier years of high school, I worried. A lot. I worried about grades, about test scores, about hard classes, about homework, about taking the ACT or the SAT, about applying to colleges and scholarships, about being involved at school and handling all the various activities.

You know, it's funny, all the worrying we do, when God is waiting with a warm smile to assure us that He will work it out. How many bloodshot eyes and wrinkled foreheads I could have avoided if I had known then what I know now—my God is big enough to make up for where I lack, and can handle every situation that comes my way. It is God's desire that I try my best, that I give my best to the schoolwork He has placed before me, but He's the first one to know my imperfection and inevitable failure. He is huge enough and mighty enough to compensate. Even if I don't do the best in a class or get the highest score on the ACT or get into the best college, God's big hands will fill the void where I lack. And I'm confident that what He has done for me, He will do for you!

People's Opinions Really Don't Matter

I have to admit, this lesson hasn't completely made it through my brain-waves, but I'm working on it! As teens, it's time we begin to let this truth penetrate our world-battered minds. People's opinions really aren't important. How right it is for us to wake every day and seek only the approval of the Lord. If we are doing what He wills, then it doesn't matter what the kids you sit beside in class think, or what your history teacher thinks, or even what your closest friends think. It's a difficult thing to look in the mirror in the morning and believe the truth that God's approval is all you need, but it *is* true, so we need to choose to believe it. Stick a piece of paper that says, "God's approval is all I need" on the bathroom mirror or in your room where you can see it every day.

What Counts Is God Stuff

With each breath that I take, every moment I'm awake, God is teaching me and showing me that what matters in this life is God stuff—the stuff we do for His kingdom. We can be involved in every club at our school, we can take all the hardest classes, we can play every sport, but are we giving God the time He deserves? I've learned that knowing God and developing an intimate relationship with Him is the first and foremost priority for our time. In the scope of eternity, what counts is the time we spend getting to know the Lord—praying, reading His Word, worshiping, fellowshiping with other believers. The time we spend reaching out to others—blessing them, encouraging them, sharing the message of God's awesome love on the cross—that is the stuff that will make it through the fire on Judgment Day! Daily quiet time is a must, and living big for Jesus at our schools, with our friends, at work, or wherever is more than worthy of our time. Let's give Him an undivided heart!

Time Spent With Family Is So Valuable

My senior year will be my last year at home. Next year, I will head out into the college world. The present is the time when I need to be cherishing the situation in which God has placed me and enjoying the relationships He has so graciously given me. The same is true for any girl who plans to head off for college—if that is you, you will never again be in such a position as you are at home. There will be few times, if any, where your bills will be paid by someone else, where your food will be cooked for you, and where you will be able to rest under the peaceful notion that authority rests entirely in someone else's hands. Relationships with parents can be tough stuff, but pray for God's help so you can pursue and enjoy this relationship.

Well, high school can be pretty difficult—schoolwork, classes, friends, guys, situations at home, expectations, and more—but as the sun rises each day and we get out of our cozy beds to live life, we have to remember who our Daddy is—that greater is He who is in us than he who is in the world. And living for Him is truly *all* that matters.

Kristie Kleinow is a student at Moody Bible Institute, majoring in communications and biblical languages. She loves learning more about Jesus, being with her family, and eating frozen yogurt!

Share Your Faith With a Friend

So, you *want* to share your faith with a friend, but you don't know what to say? Here's some help. Leading someone to Christ is as simple as A—B—C!

A—Admit. Help your friends to see that they have a need for Jesus. They have messed up (and sinned). That is what keeps them separated from God. They need to admit that they need Jesus to forgive them of their sins.

In a society that teaches moral relativism, some teens think they haven't sinned—after all, if it feels good, do it, right? Wrong! The God of the universe (who created them) has standards for them! Just take the Ten Commandments. Ask them: Have you ever dishonored your parents? Ever lied? Ever stolen anything? Ever used God's name in vain? Ever wanted what belonged to someone else? If they say "yes" to even one of these questions, they have broken God's standard and they have sinned.

B—Believe. Tell them all about Jesus so they can believe He is God's Son, sent from heaven to die on the cross to pay the penalty for their sins. Remind them that the punishment for sin is death, but Jesus came to die in their place. After He died, God raised Him back to life. New life! That's what Jesus offers them when they believe in Him.

C—Confess (and Commit). Now is the time they should confess their sins and commit their life to Jesus. Explain that to receive His free gift of eternal life they need only pray and ask Him into their hearts.

Encourage them to pray, in their own words, something like this:

Lord Jesus,

Thank You for loving me so much that You died on the cross for my sins. I realize my sin has separated me from God, so Jesus, I ask You to forgive me of my sins so that I have eternal life and can live forever in heaven with God. Jesus, I now ask You into my heart and make You the Lord and Master of my life. Fill me with Your Holy Spirit so I can live a life that honors You.

In Your name, Amen.

Now that they have started a relationship with God, encourage them to:

1. Read the Bible—the handbook to life, it will teach them all about God and help them learn how to live the Christian life.
2. Pray—simply by talking to God they can tell Him what's in their hearts.
3. Go to church—being with other people who want to know God and worship God will give them the support and encouragement they need to stay strong in Christ.
4. Tell others that they have given their life to Jesus and want to live for Him!

OK, that's the basic stuff you gotta know about leading a friend to Christ. So, be bold! Be brave! You can do it!

Mentor Friendships

Life was so confusing! I had just left my modeling career in New York and moved back to Tulsa, where my family lived. I knew the Lord had told me to do this, but I was clueless as to what should come next.

Should I do nothing? Live at home? Get an apartment? Get a job? Go to college? Find a husband? Leave for the mission field? I didn't know what God wanted! Or what I wanted (except that I wanted to do what God wanted—*whatever that was!*).

I didn't seem to be able to sort through the rubble on my own, so I consulted a special Christian friend of mine. She had been walking with the Lord longer than I had, she knew the Bible, and she was older and more mature than I was. Her godly wisdom helped me see that getting a job would help me get a productive start. Then I would have the money to get a car, so I could even drive myself to school. Several months later, when it was time to enroll in school, God opened a way for me to use some scholarship money I had earned several years earlier in pageants to pay for tuition!

The Lord used that mature Christian woman to guide me. He will often use other Christians to speak to us. Their godly advice can help us see God's plan. These special people are often called "mentors," a word that means a trusted counselor.

Proverbs 11:14 says, "Where there is no guidance, the people fall, but in abundance of counselors there is victory" (NAS). If you have no guidance, you will flounder and be easy prey for Satan, so seek the counsel of a godly woman you can trust, someone who will cheer you on and coach you in the game of life. This should be a person who can help you sort through the Bible, your prayer impressions, your circumstances, and your emotions so you can discern God's guidance in every situation.

Pray and ask the Lord to show you who could be a mentor to you. It could be your mom, your pastor's wife, your youth director, a coach, a teacher, an aunt, a Campus Life or Young Life leader, or a mature Christian from your church. Use this list as a guideline. Keep your spiritual eyes open. God will show you the right person to be your "older and wiser" friend!

Mentor Matchups

Look for these special qualities in your mentor:

- ♥ A woman who is committed to the Lord
- ♥ A woman who loves and cares for you
- ♥ A woman who is older in years and mature in her faith
- ♥ A woman who will pray with you
- ♥ A woman from whom you can receive discipline or correction
- ♥ A woman who you trust will have your best interests at heart
- ♥ A woman who will be honest and tell you the truth (even if it's not what you want to hear)
- ♥ A woman who knows you well, who can help you see your natural talents and gifts from God
- ♥ A woman who will encourage you and challenge you to become the *best you* that you can be
- ♥ A woman you admire and respect (and for the right reasons—not just because she has great hair or wears cool shoes)
- ♥ A woman who can help you pinpoint how God might be working in your life

Once you have identified a good mentor matchup, write her a note telling her what she means to you and what you admire about her. Then ask her to pray about being your mentor!

Groovy Stuff With Girlfriends

Dare to be inclusive! Invite a slew of girls over—some you've known forever, some you want to know better—and do some fun things. You can create new memories with new and old friends. Here are six ideas to get your creative juices cranked up!

☺ Pile into a car and go to the grocery store. Have each person buy five dollars worth of whatever she wants. Come back and create a meal with whatever ingredients you have collected! Bon appétit!

☺ Have a bigger, better, scavenger hunt. Divide into teams. Go to the first house and ask for something simple, to get started. Continue going to different houses, asking each homeowner for something bigger or better than the item you collected from the last house—watch them get in on the fun! Have all teams meet back in one hour to show off their treasures. (Only do this in a safe neighborhood or only go to homes of those you know.)

☺ Plan a video party. Round up a few camcorders and make a list of zany things each group must catch on tape. After an hour or so, regroup and giggle your way through your exclusive viewing. You may want to award some Oscars!

☺ Host the ultimate ice cream tasting party! Purchase twenty individually packed scoops of cool flavors from your local Baskin Robbins (or whoever!). Number the bottom of the cups one through twenty. On a separate piece of paper, record the names of the flavors corresponding to each cup (don't lose this sheet). When your guests have arrived, line up the twenty flavors and let them take a teeny taste of each one and write down what flavor of ice cream they think they are tasting. When everyone is finished tasting, read the original list and see who got the most correct. Now, put the rest of the ice cream—yep, all the flavors—together into one huge bowl, add some bananas, chocolate sauce, whipped cream, and a couple of cherries on top and dive into the gigantic sundae! All together now!

☺ Create your own mini-golf course. Get eighteen large plastic cups and set them on their sides, to be the holes. Strategically set them throughout the house, adding obstacles to each hole. Now get a putter or two, some colored balls (or color some white ones), and a score sheet. The girl with the lowest score wins!

☺ Fun facts can spice up your time! Go to a bookstore and pull out a copy of the *Guinness Book of World Records*. Pile into a couple of cushy chairs and take turns guessing the correct answers to questions about the crazy things people have done.

Little Hint
A mirror reflects a man's face,
but what he is really like is shown by the kind of friends he chooses.

Help Her Hang On!
Some Do's and Dont's for Helping Your Friend
Through a Tough Time

♥ Do let her know you care. Tell her, hug her, be there! Send her a card with an encouraging Bible verse.

♥ Do spend time just listening to her talk out her feelings and hash out the situation.

♥ Do keep your advice to yourself (in most cases).

♥ Do pray for her and with her. Ask her how you can best pray for her, what she feels she needs (such as strength, wisdom, or peace). In some situations, the best way to pray is for God's will to be done, since neither you nor your friend may know what is actually best.

♥ Do take her walking or go shoot some hoops. Physical exercise can lift a person's spirits and even help her think more clearly. It won't solve the problem or heal a deep hurt, but it will release energizers into the bloodstream.

♥ Do alert a parent, pastor, teacher, or counselor if your friend talks of feeling hopeless or purposeless, or says that she has no reason to live. Your friend may be thinking of suicide. Watch for changes in her eating and sleeping patterns, a drop in grades, or a changed personal appearance.

♥ Don't tell her you know how she feels. Unless you've been through the same exact thing, you *can't* know how she feels. Besides, we all respond differently to situations. Say, "I don't understand exactly what you're going through, but I'm here for you."

♥ Don't share a similar problem with her or tell her a story about someone you know who had something similar happen! "Man, you think you have it bad, when I was in the fifth grade...." This really won't comfort your friend. It will only make her feel like you don't think her situation is any big deal.

♥ Don't tell her it will get better. As much as you both may want it, you can't peer into the future and know what is around the corner. You can, however, remind your friend that God is faithful and trustworthy. Keep her looking to God.

Girlfriend Stuff Finale

OK, admit it.

You *need* friends! You were not created to be an isolated, independent, island! God designed you with the need to interact and connect with others. Especially with other *girls*. After all, girls are the best at understanding and appreciating each other. They often think alike, act alike, dress alike, crush alike (remember I already told you crushing on the same guy at the same time is a major friendship buster).

The relationship you develop with your girlfriends affects every day of your life. Hopefully for the *rest* of your life. Forever friends will enhance your life in ways you can't see right now. Yet *now* is the time to cultivate close-knit connections.

It is so worth the time and effort required.

Does it come easy for you? Do you automatically feel comfortable meeting new faces? Or is it work for you? Do you clam up because you are shy or because you've been hurt in the past and aren't looking forward to a repeat performance?

Whatever your situation, I urge you to put the do's and dont's in this chapter into practice right away. Go ahead. Be a good listener, be loyal, be inclusive, be an encourager, be forgiving, be helpful. Make a pact with your best buds to stick together through thick and thin, tears and laughter, broken dates and crushed dreams!

The Ya-Ya Sisterhood has nothing on you and *your* gal pals! You will be forever friends!

God Stuff

From Who He Is to What He Does to Where He's Leading You, Here's Some Important Stuff You Gotta Know About God!

God's Got a Plan

My husband was Mr. Romance early in our dating life. He poured on the charm trying to woo me. On our second date, Bill planned a picnic at the lake. He packed the hot dogs, drinks, potato chips, and all the fixin's—even remembered the blanket to sit on (no charcoal though; he used the ol' "rub the sticks together" trick—boy, was he trying to impress me).

After a wonderful dinner of burned wieners under the stars, we headed home. On the way, we pulled over (don't get excited) to check out the sights. They were guaranteed to be grandiose, according to the scenic overview sign: a night view of the city lights reflecting on the flowing ripples of the lake.

Bill was far more into it than I was. He climbed over the protective railing and proceeded to lean way out over the edge of the overhang. We're talking cliff here!

Now, I'm not adventurous, and Bill was beginning to sense it. Though he tried, he was unable to coax me over the railing. I was lagging back, hugging a boulder, totally unnerved. I didn't want to accidentally slip off the edge and fall to my doom (hey, I saw *The Lion King*, I know what can happen). I was totally satisfied with just a peek at the view. Better yet, buy me a postcard! You think I sound like a chicken, don't you? Well, I am! And I accept the fact that I'm a chicken. But that's another story.

Back to the view.

Just to please my newfound prince, I did venture to the railing. I even sat on it. He was right. I could see for miles! A bird's-eye view. Down the lake and up the lake! Panorama perfection!

God's view is like that. From where He sits, He can see our entire lives. He sees the past, present, and future. He already knows His plans for us up ahead. God sees the big picture!

During your teen years, questions about identity begin to surface: Who am I? Why am I here? Does my life have a meaning, a purpose? What does God want from me? What does He want me to do with my life? These are important questions. It's even more important that you get the right answers.

Does God have a plan, a will, a direction for you? Yes! The Bible tells us that God made us and designed us. He scheduled each day of our lives before we were even born (see Psalm 139:13-16). Yeah, that's great! But how can you know what His will is?

First, understand that God's will is in two parts. He has a general will for all of His children that He clearly lays out in His Word (the Bible).

These are things God tells us right up front. These are absolutes. No-foolin'-around-type things. These apply to *all* of His kids. For instance, you'll be wasting your words if you're wrestling with God over whether or not it's OK if you sleep with your boyfriend. All the rationale in the world won't change the fact that God has already laid out His guidelines for premarital sex in His Word. His answer? No!

God also has a specific will—something special just for you. No one can tell you exactly what this is, except God Himself! As you seek Him and develop a close, intimate, love relationship with Him, by studying His Word, you will learn to sense God's leading in every area of your life.

If you are expecting God to reveal your whole life to you all at once, you'll be disappointed. He doesn't work that way.

God unrolls His specific plan like a scroll. He shows us bits at a time, and only at the right time. He'll tell you what you need to know for the moment. He won't lay it out all at once.

Why does He do it that way? He has His reasons. One reason is that He loves you. He wants what is best for you. If He showed you everything all at once, it might freak you out! Another reason is that He is working on you. He may not show you what to do or answer your request immediately because He's taking you through a learning process of some sort. He's preparing your heart so you'll be ready to accept His plan when He shows it to you. While I was modeling in New York, if God had suddenly told me I was going to be a pastor's wife instead of gracing the covers of magazines or up on the "Big Screen," I wouldn't have taken it very well. Instead, in His wisdom and gentleness, He showed me the true value of life and convinced me I had more to give this world than a smile on a magazine cover. He did this *before* He told me to pack my bags and head home for the new life He had planned. Smart guy!

Another reason God unfolds His plan for us piece by piece is that it forces us to stay tight with Him. Oh, how He longs for us to come to Him, to be in His presence. He loves to be with us. It's when we're tuned in that we can hear Him speak. And trust me, He cares about you and does have a plan for your life, even now as a teen. So put your hand in God's hand! He will show you the way!

For God is at work within you, helping you want to obey Him, and then helping you do what He wants.

PHILIPPIANS 2:13

I will instruct you (says the Lord) and guide you along the best pathway for your life; I will advise you and watch your progress.

PSALM 32:8

Little Hint

God's overall will for you is ...

- To become Christlike by developing the character of Jesus (see Romans 8:29)
- To glorify God in what you do and say (see 1 Corinthians 6:20; Colossians 3:17)
- To tell others how to become part of God's family (see Matthew 28:18-20)

The Good Side of Bad

Lee was eighteen when a coworker invited her to his house. She thought it was odd when the other guests never showed up. The cruel and secret intention of her host was revealed when he attacked and raped her. She soon found out she was pregnant. Her parents didn't believe she had been raped and kicked her out of the house. She gave her baby up for adoption, praying for a wonderful and warm Christian home. Twenty years later she got an unexpected phone call. It was her daughter! She had been raised by a wonderful Christian couple but wanted to find her birth mother. Now they enjoy a close, loving, Christ-filled relationship.

True story.

Here's another one.

Aria's mom was killed in an automobile accident when Aria was in junior high. She had never been close to her dad, but now she was forced to interact with him. She had always despised how he pushed her into sports. Now she forced herself to go along with it, but to her surprise she found that the physical workouts helped her deal with her grief over her mom and kept her dad off her back.

She tried out for the softball team. It turned out she was good. Really good. Eventually it gave Aria and her dad something to talk about. It helped build their relationship, and she eventually got an athletic scholarship to a Christian college. She even got to travel to Mexico during the summer breaks, using softball as a witnessing tool. The first time she led someone to Christ was a thrill!

Is it possible that there can be a good side of bad? Can there really be a positive purpose for suffering? Yes! In fact, God is an expert at bringing good out of bad. This is something about God that you've just gotta know!

Romans 8:28 assures us that "all that happens to us is working for our good if we love God and are fitting into His plans." That doesn't mean that everything that happens to us is good, but that God can make something good out of it.

We may not understand why we suffer, and we will not be able to control every single thing that happens to us. Yet, if we love the Lord and aim to do His will, He can turn pain and misfortune into opportunities for growth. What possible good can be born from bad?

Hang with me and we'll take a look.

Positive Products of Suffering

1. Suffering teaches us to be sensitive and compassionate, able to comfort others who are going through hard times (see 2 Corinthians 1:3-5).

2. Problems and trials teach us to be patient, which leads to strong character (see Romans 5:3-4).

3. God can use negatives to create in us the positive qualities of Jesus (see Colossians 3:10; Romans 8:29; Galatians 5:22).

4. Crises can cause us to reevaluate our lives and recognize our need for God (see Job 2:7-10).

5. Tough stuff can test and develop our faith so we will be pleasing to God and able to withstand the storms of life (see James 1:2-4; Hebrews 11:6).

Convinced? Suffering really can become a meaningful, purposeful experience if we allow the Lord to weave it into something beautiful. In the weaving of our lives, the Lord uses the dark threads of hard times to complement the colorful threads of good times. Together they create a brilliant design that otherwise would not be possible. So, trust Him. Offer Him your hurts. See what He can create. He's an incredible artist.

My First Love:
What's It Like to Have a "True Love"? Just Ask Natalie Lloyd!

I was trying to decide between a cherry Coke and a Dr. Pepper when she slipped up behind me, almost causing me to drop the Frappucino in my hand (I was thirsty, OK?). "Why, Natalie," my mom's friend exclaimed loudly, "you look so pretty! Do you have a boyfriend?"

I laughed and thought of trying to find a creative way to say "No." I thought of, *I'm still waiting for the right one.* Or, *I don't really want to date right now.* And, *I'm trying to focus on my relationship with God.* Or, *guys aren't exactly beating down my door.* But all that would have taken too long. Before I could stammer, "No," she leaned in closer with a big smile.

"There's something different about you. Are you in love?"

The Object of My Affection
When I started my car, a praise CD kicked in, and as usual, I chimed in as loudly as I could. I love praising God in my car (so far it hasn't impaired my driving). That day as I drove through cold mountains and past empty trees, a very special thought came to me. *I was in love; I had changed.*

I have found Someone who likes to be with me all the time; Someone who loves to hear my voice as much as I enjoy hearing His. Jesus is the only guy I've ever known who hasn't said the wrong thing at the wrong time (and the only one who doesn't stop talking to me when *I* do). He thinks I'm beautiful. In His eyes, I'm just as cute when I throw on an old T-shirt and faded jeans as when I dress up to go out.

I have never felt as accepted anywhere as when I'm with Him. I don't need to rattle off a list of achievements. I don't even have to be concerned about my "chirpy Southern accent." He loves the real me. I am so incredibly far from perfect, but He doesn't mind! He's crazy about me.

When I'm heartbroken, He holds me. When I'm excited, I run to Him as fast as possible to share my news with Him. I can almost feel Him smiling (even though He knows what's happening, it's so sweet that He still loves to hear it).

The Real Secret
I'm going to be real honest with you about something, because I really wish someone had shared this with me a few years ago.

We're told over and over in God's Word that Jesus loves us. In Him we can find satisfaction, joy, hope, and peace, and we can enjoy His presence. Yet I never really thought that I could be more satisfied just by being with Him than I could be by other things—be it the perfect guy, being the center of attention, or even being beautiful. I believed *in* God, but I didn't *believe* Him. I was missing out.

What we have with Jesus is a real relationship. The more time we spend with our Savior, the easier it becomes to hear His voice, listen to His desires for our lives, and just have fun with Him! It saddens me to be around girls who *have* to have a boyfriend, because I know another person will never make them complete. Only God can do that! There's a definite joy that comes in knowing God personally, and it's absolutely incredible.

The Romantic

Don't let this get out, but I'm more romantic than I like to admit. Seeing a couple kissing in movies doesn't gross me out the way it did when I was younger. I sometimes find myself unconsciously flipping through a bridal magazine in the store, wondering just how it got in my hand. I try to imagine how it will feel to be a mom, or what I'll think when I finally know that I'm with the one guy God plans for me to spend the rest of my life with.

Yet Christ is also a romantic. He's writing a love story much better than those cheesy movies we pop in the VCR. His love is more personal than a card or a pink heart. His grace is more abundant than we can even imagine. His love is true love. Love isn't a feeling that overtakes us when someone walks in the door; rather, it's an honest and heartfelt commitment, a dedication, a willingness to keep loving, even when someone may not love us back.

Please know this: Our God is the God of second chances. He died for us while we were still His enemies. He promised us eternity with Him, and He also promises to be with us, loving us every step of the way. He is the Guy of our dreams. Jesus isn't some "spiritual boyfriend" waiting for Friday night movies. He's the Lord and Savior who knows our dreams, yet dreams much bigger. Don't lose heart. In His eyes, you are so beautiful and so treasured.

Something probably is a little different about me now. Sure, I may dress a little cuter or flip my hair out a little differently. But that's not what people are noticing. They're noticing a confidence that comes from my relationship with Christ. When you start to trust God and find your worth in Him, it changes more than just the inside of you! I find a little more joy each day, and the reason is simple ... I'm in love.

Love the Lord your God with all your heart, and with all your soul and with all your mind! Keep God #1 in your life and let Him be your first love (see Matthew 22:37; Revelation 2:4)!

Natalie Lloyd is the 1999 BRIO Girl who has a sweet southern drawl to match her sweet smile. She currently writes a monthly devotional in BRIO Magazine for her "In Step" column. She is a senior at Carson Newman College, in Jefferson City, Tennessee, majoring in communications.

Learning to Dance

It almost looked like a dance. An effortless waltz. The seagull I was watching soared up, glided sideways, dipped low—a little to the left, then to the right. He actually looked as if he was having fun! Bowing to the wind's beckoning to ride, accepting the invitation with great delight.

It's an interesting thing, the wind. You can't see it, but you can see its effects. You can see evidence of its existence. The same is true for the Spirit of God. Jesus said in John 3:8: "The wind blows where it wishes and you hear the sound of it, but do not know where it comes from and where it is going; so is everyone who is born of the Spirit" (NAS). We cannot physically see the Holy Spirit, but we can see evidence that He exists because we can see the results of His work in our lives and the lives of others.

Is it possible that when we are in step with the Holy Spirit, when we allow Him to lead, when we accept His invitation by placing our hands in His, that we will experience the dance of our lives? Could it be the most exciting, most joyous, most romantic, most adventurous existence ever?

Yes!

And the best part is that you *will* see Him working in your life. This will strengthen your faith and give you confidence to dance even more.

Pause for a second and ask yourself:

_____ yes   _____ no   Have I been dancing with the Spirit?

_____ yes   _____ no   Have I seen His working in my life?

_____ yes   _____ no   Do I truly want to dance even more?

Now, take a moment to boost your faith! Record at least three things you've seen the Spirit of God do! Big or small, it all counts. So whether He reminded you that an assignment was due, convicted you for being dishonest, or comforted you when you were upset, give Him credit here:

_____

_____

_____

_____

Girls, every day the Holy Spirit extends to you a personal invitation to take His hand, take His lead, and dance!

For all who are led by the Spirit of God are sons of God.

ROMANS 8:14

Little Hint

You are part of God's overall plan here on earth. God uses people to get His will accomplished. Therefore, there is something special He wants you to do. What if you say no? What if Jesus refused the cross or Noah refused to build the ark? Suppose Paul wouldn't preach the gospel to the Gentiles? What if the disciples had kept Jesus a secret? You will never know how God plans to use you if you say no. Pray now, committing yourself to His will for your life.

Pray, Pray, Pray!

A few months ago, my husband, Bill, and I got away for a little R & R. We soon discovered, however, that we had failed to inform the neighboring wildlife that we were trying to sleep in. We woke to an annoying little tap, tap, tap. We got out of bed and sleepily sought out the source. To our amazement, sitting on the sill of the guestroom window was a very small gray bird, pecking his dark little beak on the glass. Persistent little guy.

I'm sure there was a logical explanation for the tapping. Did he want in? Was he seeing his reflection? Was there a secret Morse code thing going on amongst the birds? We couldn't figure it out! The tapping continued.

Since we were up, a morning jog seemed in order (OK, Bill wanted to jog, I wanted coffee and a doughnut). When we returned, we instantly heard the tap, tap, tap. We went to look at our visitor, and yes, there he was, and he had brought a friend! A tapping duet! Oh, joy! Double persistence!

I couldn't help but think of Jesus' parable about the man who kept knocking on his neighbor's door until he received what he asked for, until he found what he sought, until the door was opened—which it finally was! Jesus uses this story to encourage us to be persistent in prayer. To be diligent in asking, seeking, and knocking. Just like the little bird, continue to tap! And don't do it alone. Go for the duet! Invite a friend to take your request before the Lord as well. Then trust that at just the right time, the window of heaven will open and you will receive the answer. Persistence in prayer pays off!

For everyone who asks, receives; and he who seeks, finds; and to him who knocks, it shall be opened.

LUKE 11:10, NAS

Me? A Missionary?

As a young girl, Amy Carmichael looked into the bathroom mirror at her big brown eyes and wished that they were blue.

She asked her mother if she thought that God could change the color of her eyes. Her mom replied, "Amy, God can do anything He wants to do."

So Amy prayed very hard that night for God to change her big browns to baby blues. Then she went to bed. She was so excited she could barely sleep.

The next morning she shot out of bed and ran to the mirror. And guess what happened?

Nothing!

At first Amy was pretty peeved at God. She didn't understand why He had chosen not to grant her request. Was it too much to ask? Was it too hard for Him? Amy's wise and loving mom told her, "Amy, God must have a plan for you and those brown eyes."

Amy Charmichael was born on December 16, 1867, in the village of Millisle on the northern coast of Ireland. She was raised in a devout Christian family and fell in love with Jesus at an early age.

As a teen she had an experience that shaped her values.

One Sunday afternoon on the way home from church, Amy and her brothers came upon a frail woman who was all bent over a heavy bundle. Her brothers lifted the load, and Amy helped to support the woman as she walked. Several members of Amy's church had passed by, seeing the poor woman, yet none had stopped to help. Amy was furious. She was frustrated with the self-righteous attitude of her fellow church members.

In her heart, Amy knew what really mattered in life. She said, "Nothing could ever matter again but the things that were eternal." The things that had lasting value.

Amy was serious about that.

On January 13, 1892, Amy was called to be a missionary. Two words from the Lord were planted deep in her heart. They were, *"Go Ye!"*

She knew the meaning of those words because she knew her Bible.

They didn't mean go ye into the kitchen to have a milk shake.

They didn't mean go ye into the mall and shop till you drop.

They didn't mean go ye to a party and kick it up with your friends.

They meant go ye into all the world and share the gospel—the Good News about Jesus Christ.

God said "Go Ye," and so she did!

Where did she go? India!

Wow! That's taking that go ye stuff pretty seriously!

God used Amy to rescue young girls who had been used for sexual rituals by the Hindus. Amy would often dress like a native, with a veil across her face, allowing her to sneak into the Hindu temples and get the young girls. Dressed in that garb, she wasn't recognized. In fact, all you could see were those *big brown* eyes! The same color eyes as the natives!

Think of it. If Amy Carmichael had had *blue* eyes, God could not have used her to save hundreds of children from a horrible life. She would have been recognized and arrested.

God had a plan for Amy and those brown eyes!

God has a plan to use you, too! And He will use you just the way He designed you—brown eyes, blue eyes, green eyes, tall, short, blonde, or brunette!! God wants to use *you* to communicate His love and grace to a lost and dying world.

"Go ye" are two words that God says to each of His children.

We are all called to tell others the Good News that Jesus has come into the world to rescue them from the penalty of their sins and that He offers them new life, eternal life from this moment on.

"Go ye into all the world and preach the gospel to all creation."

He calls you to go to your school, your cheerleading squad, your athletic team, your after-school job, your neighbor, your family. Go to the nursing home, the homeless shelter, the hospital, the prisons.

Go and tell them about God's Son!

You gotta know that God wants you to *go!*

Will you?

 Anyone who calls upon the name of the Lord will be saved. But how shall they ask him to save them unless they believe in him? And how can they believe in him if they have never heard about him? And how can they hear about him unless someone tells them?

ROMANS 10:13-14

Little Hint

Ever get so into everything *you* have to tell God that you forget there might be something *God* wants to *tell* you? Prayer is a two-way conversation! You talk, God listens, then God talks and *you* listen! Too many times we chat our heads off then grab our backpacks and head out the door (or grab the remote and get lost in the TV). Girlfriend, God is saying to you, "Hello? Hello? You know that huge problem you just told me about? I have an answer for you. Hello?"

Enhance your relationship with God by staying put and listening. Open the Bible—God uses it to speak to you and answer your prayers. God wants to talk to you about the issues on your heart. Shhh! Listen!

I'd Like You to Meet My Son

God, the heavenly Father, has a Son that He is so proud of! He wanted you to meet Him so much that He sent Him to earth to make your acquaintance!

Why does God want you to know His Son, Jesus? What makes Him so special? How will knowing Him make a difference in your life?

To find the answers, let's take a closer look at who Jesus really is. Here's some stuff you've just gotta know about Jesus:

1. He is the *bread* that nourishes our souls and provides for our daily needs (see John 6:35).
2. He is the *light* that chases away the darkness in our lives (see John 8:12).
3. He is the *shepherd* who lays down His life for the sheep (that's us!), protecting them, leading them, healing them (see John 10:11; Psalm 23).
4. He is the *vine* that connects us to God and fills us with His Spirit and His joy (see John 14:7; 15:1).
5. He is the *door* to salvation, opening the way for us to have our sins forgiven. This saves us from the punishment of those sins (life in hell) (see John 10:9; 1 John 1:9).
6. He is the *way* to heaven, and when we believe in Him, we spend eternity with God (see John 14:6).
7. He is the *friend* we can trust, depend on, and confide in (see John 15:15).

No wonder God wants you to meet Jesus! He is the answer to your heartfelt desires and your deepest needs. Knowing Him will change your life!

Little Hint

Nothing catches God by surprise.

Yes, Lord, Yes!

The Atlantic City Convention Center rocked with thunderous applause as Miss America 1995 was announced. The judges had selected an amazing young woman from Alabama named Heather Whitestone. She had amazed them with her grace and charm. Amazed them with her encouragement to youth. And amazed them with her inspiring ballet performance. She especially had amazed them because she was deaf.

Heather had suffered a rare reaction to a childhood vaccination when she was just eighteen months old. The medicine that saved her life left her deaf.

During her high school years, Heather really struggled with being deaf. She prayed that God would allow her to hear again. Yet that was not His choice for her. Through the Bible, God showed Heather that He had a reason for everything and that she could trust Him. Why?

He is sovereign. He is the one who rules and reigns over heaven and earth, even over our lives. Here is how the Scriptures refer to God:

> Mighty One, Faithful, Rock,
> Almighty, Judge, Most High,
> King, Powerful, Holy One

God is the headman! In an army, He's the Commander. In a business, He's the C.E.O. In a ball club, He's the owner and head coach.

Eventually Heather made peace with God's sovereign plan. When I interviewed Heather for a BRIO article, she shared, "I told God I don't choose to be deaf, but if He can use my deafness to change other people's lives, then I will be deaf for Him." She went on to say that she knew that if she had turned away from God in anger and bitterness, she might never have been crowned Miss America.

Heather's life is a perfect example of God's sovereignty. He allowed her deafness in order for her to be a powerful witness for Him. It was His plan for Heather to be deaf. It was His plan for Heather to be Miss America.

Heather's response is an example for each of us. She accepted God's plan and allowed Him to use her life as He desired.

Say "yes" to God's sovereignty. Say "yes" to His plan! Say "yes" to the things He brings into your life! Each of these things is vital if you are truly seeking God in your life.

If you say "no" to God and dig in your heels against Him, you'll have no peace. You'll end up being bitter and resentful. The love relationship God desires with you will rot away.

It's true that you won't *understand* everything our sovereign God allows or directs you to do. You won't *like* everything, either. Yet *other* things will bring you great joy and gratitude. Your life will overflow with a peace you never thought possible!

Little Hint
Nothing comes into your life that hasn't first filtered through God's fingers of love.

OK, God, Truth or Dare?

In the wee hours of a sleepover with my friends I'd always break out in a sweat when someone wanted to kick off a game of "Truth or Dare." It's not like I had much to hide, but I never trusted the questions they'd ask or the dares they'd dish out. Besides, I hated to be put on the spot!

Not God. Being put on the spot is one of His specialties.

Can you imagine playing the game with Him?

"OK, God. Truth or dare?" you ask.

"Truth," He says confidently.

OK, you knew He'd say that. He always chooses truth. Why? *Because He always tells the truth.*

God is not a man that He should lie (see Numbers 23:19).

Yet, He not only talks the truth, He *is* the truth.

"I am the way, and the truth, and the life ..." (John 14:6, NAS).

And He has carefully overseen the writing and compilation of His truths in a book called the Bible, the Word of God.

"Thy Word is truth" (John 17:17, NAS).

As His child, it's very important that you learn about and stay focused on God's truth. See, if you know what is *true*, then you will successfully detect what is false.

When Satan, the god of this world, fires a lie your way, you'll recognize it. He is the Father of Lies!

When the voices from the world's newspapers, the radio, the TV, and politicians sort of make sense, yet you feel like something's not quite right, you will be able to unmask their alluring half-truths and expose their deception.

Don't let others spoil your faith and joy with their philosophies, their wrong and shallow answers built on men's thoughts and ideas, instead of on what Christ has said.

COLOSSIANS 2:8

Our world will always promote philosophies and beliefs that are opposite to the truth, opposite to God's Word.

Why? Because Satan, the god of this world, is opposite to the God of the Word. Satan is God's enemy. He has been trying to deceive God's people with his wicked schemes and cause them to doubt God's Word since the Garden of Eden!

Don't fall for it.

The Bible tells you over and over to wise up to the wise guy; that's Satan!

So tune in and take note! Here are Satan's three main goals:

Goal One: To lie and distort the truth. John 8:44 calls Satan the Father of Lies. All he can do is lie. There is no truth in him.

Goal Two: To devour and discourage believers. In 1 Peter 5:8 it says that Satan prowls around as a roaring lion, looking for someone to pounce on and tear apart.

Goal Three: To steal, kill, and destroy. John 10:10 says it best. Satan wants to *steal* our joy, *kill* our trust, and *destroy* our relationship with Jesus. He may want to end our very lives, but Jesus said that no one could snatch us out of God's hand (see John 10:29).

Now you know Satan's goals. How does he try to achieve them? By disguising himself as a good guy with a sincere heart. The Bible says he comes as an angel of light. His schemes, lies, and temptations might look good at first glance, but they are a trap.

You can wise up to Satan's schemes by continually reading the truth in God's Word. Remember, when you know what is true, you'll be able to recognize what is false.

Little Hint

Satan has a big roar, but do not fear! The Spirit of God living inside of *you* is a super power that can out-tackle Satan anytime. Take authority over him! Resist him! Remind him who *you* are (a child of the Most High, All Powerful God, protected by your Father) and who *he* is (a fallen angel, defeated by Jesus, headed for eternal punishment in hell) (see 1 John 4:4; James 4:7-8; Matthew 28:18; 2 Peter 2:5).

Encouragement 24/7

There's a book you can read to get a word of encouragement any time you need one. It doesn't matter the time of day or night. It's always available—morning, noon, or night. It doesn't matter where you are. You can easily fit it into your backpack, on your nightstand, or in your purse. It's the Bible. It always has something wonderful to say—a direct message from God to you!

For instance ...

Lisa's life had changed so much since her relationship with God had taken a serious turn. It had happened up at camp. Away from school friends, she had had time to focus on the Lord. He had revealed Himself to her in new ways and she had rededicated her life to Him. She had vowed to make changes in her lifestyle when she returned home. She was pumped and excited!

But, uh-oh. Her friends back home did not share her enthusiasm. They bugged her about not showing up at the post-prom party, and Brian was pretty ticked at her for breaking it off with him.

Sitting in the stands at their school's varsity basketball game, she was within earshot of their crude and rude remarks. Her heart started beating hard. She could feel the pounding in her chest. She grabbed her bag and headed for the bathroom. Opening her purse, she pulled out her Bible. Then there it was. Smack dab in the middle of the third chapter of 1 Peter:

> But even if you should suffer for the sake of righteousness, you are blessed. And do not fear their intimidation, and do not be troubled (v. 14, NAS).

That was exactly what she needed to hear! She was being teased for living her life God's way, but God's Word promised that doing so would bring her blessings. She was to no longer worry about her "friends" trying to make her feel like a loser for loving God. That exact encouragement—right there, right then, spoke to her. And where did she find it? In God's Word!

It was as if heaven itself had opened up and lifted the burden right off her heart! She took a deep breath, stood a little taller, and went right back to the bleachers to enjoy the rest of the game.

Wow! That's just one verse! God's Word is loaded with great stuff to encourage you—anytime, anywhere. It is always available. Go ahead, open it up!

Thy word is a lamp to my feet, and a light to my path.
PSALM 119:105, NAS

Little Hint

There is so much people can accomplish on their own when they put their mind to it! Imagine the possibilities for a girl like you who doesn't have to rely just on her own talents and abilities. You've got God on your side! He's cheering for you! There is no challenge that will come your way that you and God together can't handle (as long as it's His will). So, go for it!

God Stuff Finale

This whole God thing is HUGE!

In fact, I truly wanted to put God Stuff as the opening chapter because God wants to be (and should be) first in your thoughts, your day, your relationships, your activities, your everything!

But never mind the first chapter, the *entire* book could have been filled with stuff you gotta know about God. He is, after all, our infinite, all-encompassing, all-wise Father.

Who could ever know everything about His plans, His sovereignty, or His purposes in our lives? In this chapter we've touched on a few of these and more. We've gotten a glimpse into this God we love and serve. I challenge you to keep looking and listening for Him. He's there. He longs to continually reveal more of Himself to you. He wants you to know *who* He is, *what* He's up to, and *where* He's leading you!

At times it may seem difficult to detect God, but trust me, He's not playing some cyber game of hide 'n seek! He's not hiding.

Keep in mind that He is revealed in a still, small voice. A gentle whisper (1 Kings 19:11-12). Therefore, get silent before Him. He's revealed in His Word, His love letter to you. So sit down, open it, read it, study it. Meet Him there. He is also revealed in nature, in His creation (Romans 1:20). Look how it speaks of His majesty, His power, His creativity!

No, our God is not hiding.

He wants us to know Him personally.

How cool is that?

Guy Stuff

From Clues to the Opposite Sex to Abstinence to
Groovy Group Dates, Here's Some Insight Into
the World of Guys 'n Stuff!

The Opposite Sex

Opposites. Things that are contrary to each other. Things that may conflict or complement each other. Things that are 100 percent completely different. Opposites!

Here's an interesting observation about opposites: they often work together to bring out the best in each other, and they often fit together just perfectly to create a single unit.

Both of these observations are true of guys and girls. In fact, the two sexes are perhaps the ultimate in opposites. They are completely different, yet God designed it that way on purpose so that they would complement each other. (Note: Every person is complete in Christ. Yet if God calls him or her to marry, the two make a complete marriage unit. God calls many people to remain single in order to fulfill the plan He has for them.)

Guys are the opposite of girls in nearly every way. Generally speaking ...

Guys have thicker skin	Girls have softer skin
Guys have longer vocal cords	Girls have shorter vocal cords
Guys have stronger muscles	Girls have higher pain tolerance
Guys can do stuff without thinking	Girls have keen insight

Guys focus on getting things done	Girls enjoy the process of doing something
Guys stay bottled up inside	Girls love to express their feelings
Guys like to do one thing at a time	Girls can juggle tasks

When you are trying to figure out why a guy did this or that, it will help you to understand that they are very different from you. Don't expect them to act like you, think like you, pray like you. You will never be able to have them totally figured out. So, don't get frustrated! Have faith! Opposite is God's plan!

To Date or Not to Date?

Kelsy is a fun girl who loves to do crazy things with her friends, hit the Del Taco drive-thru whenever possible, and wear creative decals on her nails. She is a varsity cheerleader, a record-setter on the girls' swim team, and a member of her youth group leadership team, who can be seen cruising out of the parking lot with her convertible top down and her Zoe Girl CD way up!

Kelsy's last-semester grades were a stack of straight A's. She's a responsible daughter who often takes care of her younger sister. On weekends she likes getting lost in a classic novel or meeting her girl-friends for a cappuccino (add some whipped cream, please!). She's just one of those well-rounded, really fun girls!

Now want to hear all about her boyfriend? Sorry, not possible. She doesn't have one. She doesn't date!

She made the decision her freshman year to use her high school years to develop some "girl" friends that would last her whole lifetime, instead of allowing herself to be swept up into the whole "guy" thing. What about you? Have you really thought it through?

See, just because it's sort of assumed in our society that you will date does not mean that you should. Why let others dictate your decision? You can decide on your own! You've got a brain! You are intelligent! You don't need to follow the crowd!

So, here are some things to think about. At first glance, they could sound radical to you. Old-fashioned. Too godly. Stuffy. Boring. Yet look again. Contemplate them. Write out the pros and cons of diving into the dating scene before you do it.

If you choose not to date, you can:

- ♥ Be more focused on your studies (daydreaming or hoping a guy will call you is totally distracting)
- ♥ Spend more time trying new things (go ahead, sign up for that jazz dance class or watercolor painting workshop)
- ♥ Put your energies into service projects (hey, you could start an adopt-a-grandparent program between your youth group and a local nursing home)
- ♥ Avoid the roller-coaster ride of the date-break up, date-break up pattern that most teen relationships go through (beware—that pattern may make it easier to walk out of your future marriage when things get tough)
- ♥ Steer clear of the temptation to become sexually active
- ♥ Be free from sexually transmitted diseases and an unplanned pregnancy
- ♥ Spend valuable time getting to know a very special person with whom you are going to spend the rest of your life: You!

Reasons for Going Solo

1. You can totally be yourself without worrying if your guy is impressed or embarrassed!
2. You don't have to sit through rough war flicks, or shoot 'em up

or zap 'em up movies. You can rent your favorite chick flicks anytime you want! Not to mention eating buttery popcorn by the handfuls!

3. You don't have to think about having kissable breath. Go ahead and put all the garlic, onions, or anchovies you want on your pizza!

4. You can build your self-esteem based on God's unchanging, unending, unconditional love for you.

Your turn! Have a little brainstorming session and see what you come up with. List the pros and cons here:

To Date or Not to Date

Pros   Cons

_____

_____

_____

Your conclusion:

_____

Now spend some time in prayer. Ask the Lord to reveal His heart and desires for you on this issue. Ask what His best for you would look like.

Don't copy the behavior and customs of this world, but be a new and different person with a fresh newness in all you do and think. Then you will learn from your own experience how His [God's] ways will really satisfy you.

ROMANS 12:2

Only God can meet the inner needs of the real you!

Little Hint

It's a really good idea not to hang out with guys who are older than you. It's very possible that they have more than a movie or a game of Monopoly on their mind!

Boost That Boy's Bounce!

Ever notice that some guys seem to have a bounce in their step? It's sort of like having an air of confidence, a strong feeling of assurance, a healthy self-esteem.

Then, of course, there are those who shuffle instead of bounce. They muddle down the hall with their eyes glued to the floor. They often have some really great qualities, but they need a little encouragement to see that.

You can help!

You can make a guy comfortable being himself, and help him to like himself and to become the diamond that right now is probably in the rough! See, guys have odd ways of dealing with their insecurities— some put on the tough guy act, some go for the Mr. Cool look, others get into the laid-back, what's-up approach to everything. Girls are pretty keen about seeing through the facades and picking up on their potential. Girls can sense that there's something more to those males, something deeper (like hidden treasures). They catch a glimpse of qualities that could make these guys shine like sparkling gems, stand tall like the mighty oak, soar like the proud eagle, and ... OK, OK, you get the picture, right?

Of course you can't single-handedly turn a guy into a gem, an oak, or an eagle, but you can help him feel a little less self-conscious when he trips on his shoelace, dribbles on his shirt, spits when he talks, forgets to zip up his fly, loses his car keys, gives the wrong answer in class, or gets benched during the big game!

Just follow these seven simple steps to boost the bounce (and be a genuine friend) to the guys in your life.

1. Accept his physical uniqueness. In other words, don't talk about his body! Whether he's a slim Jim or a beefy Brad, whether he's got humongous ears or bushy brows, he is still a one-of-a-kind, original handiwork of God. Appreciate his individual look!

2. Cut out the comparisons. Just as girls hate to be compared to supermodels, actresses, or even their sisters, guys don't like the comparison thing either. Just let him be himself!

3. Overlook obvious oddities. Trust me, though he may act totally oblivious, he probably already knows he has hat hair or a gigantic zit on his chin. And even if there is dried mustard on his right cheek or lettuce hanging off his braces, control yourself. Let his buddy break the news to him, not you!

4. Come to his rescue. Even at the risk of the guy thinking you like him (as in LIKE him), it's a real boost for him to have you defend him when he's being trashed. See, a person's feelings and reputation are valuable. So, if you can set the record straight or stick up for him, do it!

5. Respect his opinions. Some girls feel cool and in control when they blast a guy's ideas. Yet they are really communicating total disrespect for him. If he trusts you enough to share his opinions, responding with a thoughtless "that's a stupid way to feel" will either tick him off or send him into a shell. Even if what he says is a little "out there," be mature by asking him to explain his thoughts or at least by not laughing in his face.

6. Don't be nosy. Guys can turn green when you start asking them too many personal questions. It takes time for them to trust a girl and to "test the waters" of your trustworthiness before they open up. And really, really don't probe around to find out who they like or why

they aren't going out with anyone. After all, being "girlfriendless" is not a disease. It's a good decision (in my opinion). Guys are already loaded with active hormones. It's better that they keep them in line rather than feeling pressure from you to be dating someone!

7. Encourage him. Just like girls, guys struggle with their self-esteem. When he puts himself down, turn it around. Build him up! Be a real friend by helping him to see his potential.

Little Hint

Have some dating defenses tucked up your sleeve! When asked if you're going out with someone (and you're not), try, "I'm dating Brad Pitt, but we're keeping it a secret!" Or if asked why you're not going out with someone, respond with something like, "Because I'm in love with Ben Affleck." Choose the hunk of your choice!

Say What?

I remember the Christmas I was going to give my dad the clock I made for him in junior high. This was a big deal, not just because I had personally cut it out and then sawed, glued, and nailed the thing together, but because I had done it at a great expense.

See, I was one of only three girls in a woodworking class full of guys. And in junior high that is not a cool thing. I was mocked, ridiculed, teased, and embarrassed more times than I want to admit. One particular day I got a whammy. A couple of geeky boys made it their personal mission to come over and announce to me something I already knew: You have a moustache! (Oh, Lord, why do girls have upper lip hair?)

Had I been more nervy, I would have told them that if they get lucky, perhaps when they grew up they could have one too! Unfortunately, I've never been quick on my feet with comebacks.

Most girls would have dropped the class at this point. Not me. I was determined to finish my clock and present it to my dad on Christmas morning. I didn't care what other people were saying about me, or the persecution it was causing me. I was focusing on Christmas morn.

Being teased about your appearance (or anything else, for that matter) can really hurt. It can make a perfectly happy girl suddenly feel insecure.

Guys tease. Guys can be cruel. Guys can be fickle. Yep. They will often say unkind things to girls to whom they are attracted. Go figure! They may find it too intimidating to be honest with their feelings, especially if they are uncomfortable handling their emotions toward girls. So, they tease. Some of their teasing crosses the line, and it hurts.

What's a girl to do?

Let It Go

When you choose to hold a grudge, it only hurts you! Jesus teaches us to forgive, no matter how much it hurts, no matter if the person deserves forgiveness or not. When you forgive others, you are being obedient to the Lord. He will honor that!

Think of yourself as choosing to "walk" in forgiveness. Walking is a continuous action. If you stop walking, you are standing!

This suggests that we are to continually forgive others. Plus, walking is a forward motion. So, let go of their stinging comments and move forward.

Write It Down

Bottling up your fractured feelings can lead to an emotional explosion. So, start by letting it all out in a journal. Record exactly what you feel and why you feel that way.

Talk It Out

Share your feelings with a mature Christian friend, trusted youth leader, or parent. Sometimes just talking about it helps a ton. Plus, when you share your burden with a friend, it suddenly appears smaller.

So, let it go, write it down, talk it out. And pray that next time you'll have a really great comeback. (Just kidding!)

All Wrapped Up
Become Passionate About Purity With Lisa Velthouse, 2000 BRIO Girl

"You've gotta see this!" he said, excitedly entering the house. My dad had just returned from running errands on a Saturday afternoon, and he was obviously thrilled about something. As he pulled a small bag from his coat pocket and handed it to me, a boyish grin spread across his entire face. Looking inside the bag, I immediately recognized the shape and velvety covering of a jewelry box. I took in a quick breath of air and looked up with shock, because I was almost certain of what the container held. My suspicion was verified with only one statement. "I had it redone," he said.

It had been almost two years since the diamond had fallen out of my mom's wedding band, and her ring had been tucked away ever since. In its place she wore another ring, but she often revealed to me that the replacement "just didn't look right," compared to the original. My dad had always known that his wife missed her wedding ring, but for a time other financial matters had kept him from being able to repair the diamond's setting. When finally able to do so, he was nothing less than elated.

It was late December, and my dad planned to give the ring back to my mom by placing it under the Christmas tree with our other presents.

He took extra care, though, to make it clear to everyone that this gift was special. Take, for example, the wrapping process. I'm not sure that my dad could have wrapped that present if his life had depended on it. Something about the anatomy of his fingers is disastrous when combined with tape, and the mechanics of curling ribbon seem to be a complete mystery to him. So, wisely, he left the wrapping up to me—sort of. Actually, he made me do all the work, while he supervised. Like an excited little puppy, he stayed at my heels the whole time—choosing the best paper design and the best curling ribbon. He even picked a piece of lint off the jewelry box. When the ring had finally been packaged to his complete satisfaction, my dad picked out a gift tag (matching, of course) and wrote, "To Faye, With Love From Ben." Then, he tenderly carried the gift over to our tree and placed it among the others.

On Christmas Day, as my mom pulled loads of curling ribbon from the top of her boxed wedding ring, I stole a glance at my dad and couldn't help but smile at what I saw. It meant so much for him to be able to give the perfect gift to his bride that there were traces of tears in his eyes. Moments later her eyes glistened too. The perfect gift. Protected. Packaged. Presented at the perfect moment.

For as long as I can remember, people have described sexual purity to me by comparing it to a gift—a priceless gift that I can give to my husband someday. Numerous times I have been taught about the value of waiting to have sex until I'm married, and I've heard countless lectures and sermons about abstinence. In all of my training, though, one thing was missing: I had not been taught anything about wrapping paper, that special covering that makes the gift even more exciting.

Two years ago I graduated from high school as a girl who had never been kissed and who had never been asked to go out on a single date. In fact, my only experience with romance came from a roller-skating party "relationship" in the fourth grade. To say the least, I was inexperienced in matters of love—and, as far as I could tell, that was one of the worst things for which a girl could ask. I went off to college and was more than ready to gain some familiarity with dating. I couldn't wait for my love story to begin, and I kept my eyes open for a young man who would accept a piece of my heart. As my freshman year unfolded, though, I stayed in what seemed to be an all-too-familiar situation for me: single. The dates that I had looked forward to for so long were still not happening, and my lips remained as unkissed as they had always been. For a time, my single status really bothered me, but the more I thought about it, that opinion began to change. Through time I realized that my inexperience with guys was not an entirely bad thing—in reality, there were a lot of good parts to it. Even though it seemed like I had been waiting ages (and ages!) for love to come my way, I began to understand that my life was already incredibly romantic. Yes, it was true that my heart had never been shared, but it was also true that my heart had never been broken.

Even though I hated the fact that I had never been kissed, it gave me the freedom to choose which guy got that all-important first smooch. (I could wait until the moment was just right.) I was delightfully surprised to realize what a blessing it was to have sexual purity that remained as it had always been: perfectly wrapped up, with all the bows and ribbons still attached to the top of the package. I am so grateful that my view on this has changed! Someday, when I find the right guy, I will have the option of giving my whole heart to him—because nobody else has a piece of it. Unlike so many of my peers, all my starry-eyed hopes and dreams can still be found in a nicely packaged bundle, simply waiting for a great young man to come along and open them.

Imagine for a moment that you could give your heart—all of it—to just one person. Try to picture what it would be like to share not only your sexual purity but all of your romance with the man of your dreams. What a blessing, what a gift that could be! There are countless things that have the potential to make your love story beautifully elaborate, attractive, and special. The kisses, hugs, secret smiles, touches, hopes, and dreams that you have to share can be the wrapping paper of your sexual purity. Don't be quick to give such things to just anybody—save the best wrapping for the best man.

Abstinence from sex before marriage is the perfect thing to give to your spouse, but like most other gifts, it can be made even better if you wrap it up and put a bow on top. Out of love for your future husband and out of respect for yourself, seek to make your sexual purity the best and fullest it can be—a gift that you will be proud to give away some-day. Take the initiative to save certain things just for your mate, and relish the opportunity to give him one amazing present—sexual purity that's all wrapped up!

Lisa Velthouse is a twenty-year-old woman who is so excited about her first kiss that she's planning a party to celebrate it when it happens! She is a student at Indiana Wesleyan University, where she studies English and wears high-heeled shoes as much as possible.

Purity Promise

Out of obedience to God, are you committed to absti-nence—choosing not to become sexually active before your wedding night? Are you willing to set high stan-dards for yourself (such as not dating, or not kissing passionately, or not being touched inappropriately) so as to protect your purity and to keep yourself from falling into tempting situations?

If so, make it a promise! A promise to God, to yourself, and to your future Prince Charming!

The Promise

I promise before God to honor His Word by living a life of sexual purity from this day forward. I choose to be abstinent before marriage, thus saving not only my body but my whole heart for the man God chooses for me to marry.

Signed: _Andrea E. Danley_

Date: _12-10-04_

> *For God wants you to be holy and pure, and to keep clear of all sexual sin so that each of you will marry in holiness.... For God has not called us to be dirty-minded and full of lust, but to be holy and clean. If anyone refuses to live by these rules he is not disobeying the rules of men but of God.*
>
> 1 THESSALONIANS 4:3-4, 7-8

Little Hint

It is far better to endure the temporary teasing for doing what is right than to suffer the consequences of doing what is wrong.

He's So Fine

You wouldn't believe this guy I used to date. He ran a successful business and owned his own airplane. It was great. If we wanted to go to dinner at a restaurant a hundred miles away, no problem. We would just fly there!

More than I liked this guy's airplane, I liked the gifts he gave me. They made me feel special. Long-stemmed red roses, boxes of hand-made candies, and a silk blouse I'll never forget. It was beautifully decorated with sparkling beadwork. I enjoyed the romantic way this guy made me feel. Yet, there was this one small problem. He wasn't a Christian.

Wouldn't you know it, it was just when I was dating this guy that I first heard the Scripture about not being joined together or teamed up with an unbeliever. My initial reaction was to ignore it. *No big deal*, I told myself. Yet we were just a month into our relationship when the truth of God's Word slapped me in the face.

I found out—accidentally—that my Mr. Romance was dating other women besides me. I also discovered he had a nasty cocaine habit. Of course, he kept these things hidden from me because I was a "nice girl" and we had fun together.

You see, Romeo didn't share my Christian values. He lived a life and believed in things that were ungodly. I suddenly understood why it is important to date and marry a Christian. What's the harm in just dating a non-Christian, you may ask? Let me explain. When you start spending lots of time with someone, you may become romantically and emotionally attached. It's very hard to keep a clear head when your feelings are involved. You may enjoy each other's company, but when it comes to discussing meaningful issues, you won't agree. Your values and viewpoints will be different. You won't have much in common. And breaking up is hard to do!

That's exactly the point of 2 Corinthians 6:14-15: "Don't be teamed with those who do not love the Lord, for what do the people of God have in common with the people of sin? How can light live with darkness?" Christians and non-Christians are different. They're like oil and water. You can put them in the same jar and shake them vigorously, but within seconds they start to separate. No matter how hard or how long you shake, they just don't mix.

So take it from someone who has been there ... no matter how wealthy, romantic, or wonderful the guy is, see if he values Christ and the Christian lifestyle as much as you do.

It's so easy to get swept into a relationship with a guy who sweeps you off your feet! Yet, take a good hard look at who you date—his values and beliefs—before you get too attached.

Little Hint
Kisses are like diamonds—the more of them you put into circulation, the less value each of them has!

Tackling Temptations

Making an honest commitment to holding on to your virginity until marriage is *huge!* It's tough; especially when you see romance and love scenes on almost every channel as you surf.

Chances are, you'll need to call for backup support on this one! Here are a few ideas to help you stand your ground and fight off temptation when it comes your way—and it will! Be ready!

♥ If you choose to date, restrict your dating to guys who respect God's guidelines as much as you do. When you're both on the same track, the ride is smoother!

♥ Pray with your guy. Really! Bring God right into the middle of your relationship. Prayer helps fight off temptation and keeps your focus on the right stuff.

♥ Set standards in line with God's standards. Abstaining from sexual intercourse is an absolute, but what about the other stuff? It's important not to do anything that allows you or your guy to become aroused. So, create boundaries! Declare anything below the neck and above the knees off-limits—on your body as well as his!

♥ Let small talk lead to big discoveries. Yep. Concentrate on getting to know your guy on the inside! Besides, emotional intimacy is much more fulfilling than physical intimacy.

♥ More is better! Single dating often allows for situations that are tempting. Double or triple up with other friends. It's much more fun that way!

♥ Don't flirt in a come-on kind of way. Real "babes" don't have to prove they are desirable or attractive. They protect their inner beauty by saying "no" to anything that will harm the gifts God has given them, including the gift of sex.

♥ Dress modestly. Don't dress to impress, get attention, or tempt a guy.

♥ Totally avoid being alone with a guy in the dark, in an empty house, or in a parked car. Discipline yourself to be where others are around. You never tackle temptations alone. God promises to open a door of escape when temptation is getting to be more than you can handle. See it with your own eyes.

> *But remember this—the wrong desires that come into your life aren't anything new and different. Many others have faced exactly the same problems before you. And no temptation is irresistible. You can trust God to keep the temptation from becoming so strong that you can't stand up against it, for He has promised this and will do what He says. He will show you how to escape temptation's power so that you can bear up patiently against it.*
>
> 1 CORINTHIANS 10:13

God promises, but it's up to you to *look* for the escape and to *want* to escape the situation. So, pray for strength and keep your eyes open! Satan will try to tempt you to do what God does not want you to do (just like he did Eve in the Garden of Eden). Don't fall for it! Stay strong in Christ!

But sexual sin is never right: our bodies were not made for that, but for the Lord.... That is why I say to run from sex sin. No other sin affects the body as this one does. When you sin this sin it is against your own body. Haven't you yet learned that your body is the home of the Holy Spirit God gave you, and that he lives within you? Your own body does not belong to you. So use every part of your body to give glory back to God.

1 CORINTHIANS 6:13, 18-20

Little Hint

Honoring God by choosing not to compromise your standards and respecting yourself is more important than the guy you might lose if you say "no"!

Famous Couples

OK, this is how it works. I give you the guy's name and you guess the girl's! Pay close attention. There's something special I want you to notice about these well-known lovebirds. Ready? Let's go!

Romeo and ___Juliet___
Adam and ___Eve___
Mickey and ___Minnie___
George Burns and ___Gracie___
Popeye and ___Olive Oyl___
Tarzan and ___Jane___
Shrek and ___Fiona___
Abraham and ___Sarah___
Jacob and ___Rachel/Leah___
George W. and ___Laura___

Here are the answers in reverse order: Laura, Rachel, Sarah, Fiona, Jane, Olive Oyl, Gracie, Minnie, Eve, Juliet!

How did you do?

Now scan the list again very carefully. What do all the couples have in common? They were forever couples! They had forever love! In a society where being together seems to end so frequently, believe it or not, there *is* such a thing as *forever!* There *is* such a thing as saying "I do" and having it last a lifetime.

Really!

Till death do us part *is* a possibility!

It's also the plan!

God's plan!

He's the one who originated the "two becoming one" idea.

Listen to this:

A man shall leave his father and mother, and shall cleave [be joined] to his wife; and the two shall become one flesh ... they are no longer two, but one flesh. What therefore God has joined together, let no man separate.

MATTHEW 19:5-6, NAS

Now, would God ask couples to become one and stay together for life if it was impossible to do?

No.

Being together forever is very possible!

So, why the huge divorce rate, even among Christians?

Great question.

I could give you a bazillion reasons—lack of commitment, unresolved anger, refusal to forgive, openness to an affair, lack of respect, lack of obedience to God—the list is endless. Of course, these days there's just the simple "no-fault" divorce. No huge reason, just ready to move on.

If forever love is God's plan, what is the key to staying together?

I believe it is waiting patiently for God to bring the right person into your life. That means being 99.9 percent sure that God has brought the two of you together. When you have seen His hand at work to orchestrate the circumstances so you would meet, become friends, and then see His plan for you as a couple, then it will be much harder to walk away when it gets tough! (Does God forgive those who divorce? Yes, though it causes Him, the couple, the kids, and others much pain.)

When you walk down that aisle on your wedding day, you gotta know this is God's guy for you! It matters! It makes a difference!

You can have forever love.

You and your hubby-to-be can have your names go down in history! You can be a famous "forever" couple!

Little Hint

PDA. It's just not pretty. It's just not appreciated. It's just not comfortable for others. PDA (public display of affection, in case you're clueless) is best kept to a friendly high five or the flash of your gorgeous smile. Besides, too much lovey-dovey in front of others can taint your reputation and make others wonder what you do in private, when you are so expressive in public. It also makes it more tempting to take your physical relationship to the next level when you are alone. PDA? Nada!

The Rejection Remedy

You got dumped? Yes, you feel rejected. You feel embarrassed. You wonder what people will say, if anyone will ever ask you out again, if you and your "ex" will ever be friends.

Stress from breaking up can be so upsetting that sometimes people change schools, drop out, run away, get very sick, or even think about ending their lives. Let me tell you this, as one who has already been through all the dating devastations—there is life *after* a major breakup! Though you can't concentrate on anything else and your heart feels like it's ripping out, the pain, the stress, and the worries *do* go away.

Whenever you feel rejected, it's a good time to put your prayer power into effect. Tell the Lord how you feel. Allow Him to heal your hurts.

Psalm 34:18 tells us the Lord is near to the brokenhearted. He is there to comfort you, console you, ease your mind, and calm your stress. Jesus knows what rejection feels like. For Him, the ultimate rejection led to the cross. Yet, He endured it because He loved. And one person He loves is you! Reach out to Him when you hurt. His Band-Aids are the best!

Little Hint

If you are ending a relationship, do it gently. Let the guy down slowly. Be honest, but avoid being abrupt or bruising his ego. Believe it or not, guys take breakups just as hard as girls do. They cry. They get depressed. They have feelings. They often act like they don't, but they do!

Groovy Group Dates

Use these group dating ideas to create fun, safe, and exciting dates that allow you to get to know other people in unusual ways. Focus your time together on building tight friendships that are lasting!

♥ Why be bored hangin' at someone's house? Head to the mall or your local airport to do some people watchin'! Observe as you guess where they are from, where they're headed, their occupation, the type of car they drive, and what their favorite food might be!

♥ A picture paints a thousand words. Have your friends dig out their old family photo albums and gather 'round your picnic table for a ton of laughs! Use the pictures to learn new information about each other. Then locate the nearest photo booth in town, pile in, squeeze together, and get a great group shot. A cool Kodak moment!

♥ Food, food, food! Here are some ideas incorporating the world's favorite pastime: Eating!

   Fast food progressive dinner. Go to a different fast food restaurant for each of the following: appetizer, salad, soup, burger, fries, shake, and dessert.

   Throw a regressive dinner. Start with dessert and work backward. Don't forget the Tums!

   Pizza pyramids. Gather up crust, sauce, cheese, pepperoni, sausage, onions, mushrooms, green pepper, pineapple, artichokes, black olives, and anything else you can think of and build, then bake, your own pizzas. Pop in your favorite animated video as you munch away!

♥ Model madness. Have everyone chip in a few bucks to buy some challenging kits ... model airplane, car, engines, and so on. Then divide into teams and see who can complete their kit the fastest and the best. You could do the same thing using jigsaw puzzles, or build your own kites and try to make them fly.

♥ Get smart. Take up a new hobby together. Find a few similar interests and sign up for a class. Photography, ceramics, golf, cooking, cake decorating, or even a fun Bible class (yep, learning about the Bible can be a blast with the right leader and the right attitude) are some fun ideas.

♥ Get into some acting—acting kind, that is! Have a "random acts of kindness" day. Cook someone dinner, bake cookies for an elderly couple, mow a yard, clean house for a busy mom, rake leaves, or write anonymous notes to your friends, parents, teachers, and coaches telling them what you appreciate or admire about them.

Little Hint

If your parents don't like the guy that you like, there's probably a good reason! You may not be able to see clearly through your dreamy eyes, but your parents can sense things—they may be better judges of his character. Trust them!

New Beginnings

David watched as Bathsheba, the wife of another man, bathed within view of his window. He fed his desire until he allowed it to take over. With her husband away fighting a war, David took Bathsheba to his bed and, well, you know what happened. Yet he didn't stop there. When he discovered she was pregnant, he called her husband back from battle to get him to sleep with her so it would look like the child was his. The plan didn't work, so he had her husband sent to the front lines to guarantee he'd be killed. Wow! Sin after sin after sin!

But guess what?

God forgave him.

Yes, David repented. Yes, he was held accountable for his actions. Yes, he paid the high price of the painful consequences.

Yet God continued to love him and forgive him.

That's because our God is the God of second chances. He is the God of new beginnings. He lets us start over!

For many different reasons, some girls do not save themselves for their spouse. They give themselves to a guy (or guys). It's a choice. It's a choice *against* God's best plan for them.

But still, God forgives and invites them to start over.

Are you one of those girls?

Do you need a new beginning? Would you like to experience renewed virginity, pledging that from this day forward you will remain abstinent until your wedding night?

If so, then in your own words, I invite you to pray a prayer similar to this:

Heavenly Father, I humble myself before You right now, asking You to forgive me for having sex outside of marriage. Please cleanse me and make me pure once again. Fill me with the desire and strength I need to remain abstinent from this moment forward. Thank You that spiritually I am now a virgin once again, and thank You for your unending love that I am so grateful to receive. Amen.

Now what should you do?

First, forgive yourself and the guy involved. Second, break off any sexual relationships. Third, surround yourself with those who share your new commitment. Fourth, be very wise about if you should date and whom you should date. Fifth, tell others about your new promise to purity.

Above all, get into church, a Bible study, and God's Word. Fill yourself with God so you will be strong enough to make this new beginning your last.

Little Hint

True sexual freedom means that you are free from the pressure to have sex, free from potential disease, free from the fear of an unplanned pregnancy.

Guy Stuff Finale

Oh, my goodness!

Sometimes they drive us crazy. Sometimes they make us feel like princesses. Sometimes they make us so mad. Sometimes they can melt our heart with just one little grin.

GUYS!

Yes, God created them and loves them, but it doesn't nix the fact that they are so totally *different* from us girls! My goal in this chapter has been to help you grasp this concept. Hopefully, I have also challenged you to think about where you stand on guy-related issues.

For instance, dating. Is it right for you? Is it God's best for you at this time in your life? Do you see the benefits of going solo or "dating" in groups? And modesty. Are there any changes you need to make in your attire? And purity. Are you committed to saving your heart and your virginity for your future husband? Then there's just dealing with guys in general ... their teasing, come-ons, rejections, or put-downs.

I trust I've given you some valuable stuff to think and pray about.

Allow me to encourage you to keep the whole guy thing in perspective. Don't give them the power to determine your sense of personal value or attractiveness. You don't need a boyfriend to prove you are loveable. Get your kudos from God. Trust Him with the guy stuff. After all, He is the *ultimate* guy!

Grades 'n Stuff

From Study Tips to School-Time Stress to Graduation
Prep to Witnessing on Campus, Here's Some
A+ School Kinda Stuff!

Make Your Day Rock

Let's face it. Whether you like it or not, you pretty much have to do
school! Therefore, make it count. Here are ten tips for getting the
most out of your day.

1. Be on time to every class. No, really. Those tardy slips add up,
   and detention is not as fun as some say. Besides, being punctual
   shows that you respect the rules and you're responsible!

2. Submit to your teachers' authority. Don't talk back, don't challenge them, don't make wisecracks, don't roll your eyes, don't
   flip them a 'tude, don't try to bargain with them. When you're
   asked to do something, smile and do it.

3. Use your study halls wisely. Who wants to do tons of homework
   when they get home? Use your school time—when your brain is
   more awake—to cram in your homework, and you'll have more
   time to chill after the school bell rings!

4. See your teachers and coaches as humans. I know you've ques-
   tioned their origin. They may teach like aliens or coach like animals, but they are real people, just like you. They have days that
   soar, and days that crash and burn. They have pressures and

personal lives. So cut them some slack. Be nice. Give them a compliment. Say "hey" to them in the hallway. You might make their day.

5. Refuse to cheat. It's not right. It's not fair. It's not godly. It will always come back to bite you.

6. Don't be a clique chick. Fitting with the "in" crowd is not all it's "quacked" up to be. (Sorry, I couldn't help it!) Just be yourself. Make friends with lots of different kinds of girls. Have *real* friends. Those super-popular chicks are so focused on staying popular that they don't usually make good heart-to-heart girlfriends.

7. Wear comfy stuff. OK, wearing pajamas and slippers is taking it to extremes, but when you're comfortable in your clothes, your focus can be on stuff that matters—like lectures and labs and library time! It's really good to avoid those too tight, too low-cut, too short, too bare tops and such! They make you *have* to focus on yourself.

8. Bring your essentials to class. Don't forget your homework, essays, projects, paper, pens, textbooks, notebooks, and so on. But go ahead and leave your cell phone, pager, palm pilot, and CD player in your locker!

9. Eat lunch. By noon, your body and your brain need a burst of energy. Do it with nutrition! Go for yogurt, turkey and cheese on wheat, or a protein bar. You'll be glad you did.

10. Trash rude remarks, both yours and others'. Words can build someone up or tear him or her down. Be encouraging to others. And when someone shoots a cruel comment your way, duck and let it fly by. Don't let it hit your heart.

Little Hint

Homework. Grades. Cliques. Tests. Being called on in class. Giving speeches. Teachers. Detention. Flunking out. The list goes on. School, with all of its good and bad, stresses and thrills, will fill thousands of hours of your life! Whether those are upper or downer hours will depend on how you react to it all. Do keep this in mind: The Lord wants you to learn, to become wise, and to give it your best effort.

Calm Your Morning Chaos

Your day will definitely have the crazies if you think you can shower, do your hair, fix breakfast, write a speech, and study for finals—all before 7:00 A.M.! You can cut down on your morning chaos by getting organized.

Keeping tabs on test schedules, homework assignments, practice times, rehearsal dates, and work hours will help make your days sweet. It will keep you on top of your life instead of life being on top of you!

The payoff will be well worth it. Having calm, peaceful mornings (barring any unforeseen circumstances beyond your control) will send you to school feeling more pulled together. Read through these organizational ideas and apply the ones most beneficial to you. I do recommend trying new things—especially if what you have been doing has caused you to crumble in chaos!

Make a List and Check It Twice

First, get a day planner with a weekly and monthly calendar on it. Look at the month ahead of you. Make a list of activities and dates for that month. Your list will be more complete if you write things on your calendar as soon as you find out about them. Now write down the various things you need to do in preparation for each of those activities. Knowing how much preparation you need for each activity helps you determine how soon you need to start preparing in order to be ready and relaxed.

Next, evaluate the week ahead of you. Make note of the activities, dates, and times. Schedule the time to prepare for each activity. Make a detailed list of the things you need to do for this specific week. Include items such as people you need to call or go see, assignments you need to complete, items you need to purchase, and so on.

Now, you are ready to write your daily list. Are you seeing things that need to be done right away? Great! Make your list. Your daily list will keep you on track and give you a sense of direction for the day.

Prioritize

Putting your tasks in order of importance may not be necessary on your monthly list, but is essential for your weekly and daily lists! Rank the tasks from most important to least important. Most important would be things that absolutely have to get done today. Then, if the day doesn't go exactly as you expect (and it rarely does), the less important items can be transferred to tomorrow's list. Before you go to bed, or first thing tomorrow morning, make a new list.

Group Tasks Together

Another way of using your time more efficiently is to group together tasks that can be done at the same time. This is especially timesaving when you have to drive around to complete your tasks. For example, if you pass the office supply store on your way over to Brittney's to work on your history presentation, stop to pick up the markers, tape, and paper you need to make tomorrow's poster for the school dance. This is better than making two separate trips.

Nighttime Notes

Keep a pad, pencil, and a small flashlight next to your bed. When you think of the things you have to do, write them down. You can sleep better knowing you will not forget it tomorrow!

Post-It Notes

Leave yourself notes for those super important things. Stick them on your bathroom mirror or inside the front door. This minimizes your chances of forgetting to do something (even if it is on your list) or leaving something vital (like the mold-growing science project in the fridge) at home.

Be Complete

Finish one project at a time. You will cut down on clutter and mental chaos when your brain focuses on one thing at a time. So, complete that project before you start reading that novel for English class.

Unclutter Yourself

Keeping your room picked up, your bed made, and your clothes off the floor (hang 'em up or put 'em in the hamper) will make it easier to move quickly in the morning, and will reduce your chances of losing things in your room.

Workplace Wonders

File folders, paper clips, pencil holders, stackable racks—all these types of things will help you organize your desk or homework area.

Tackle Time Stealers

Beware of the terrible two "Ts" and one "C"—television, telephone, and computer. They will steal your time and throw you off schedule!

Know Thyself

When are you most alert and full of energy, ready to tackle the day's tasks? In the morning? Afternoon? Evening? Except for the tasks that have to be done at a specific time, other tasks will be completed more efficiently when your body and mind are at peak performance.

Now, pull it together and put these pointers into practice. They will help to improve your performance and calm the crazies caused by a cluttered life and mind!

Little Hint

The world's all-time number-one study tip is this: take time at the end of the day to review your notes from each class. This helps lock the information into your mind so that studying for tests is not so stressful. You will already be familiar with the material. Plus, when you review your class notes you can "take note" of the things you don't truly understand. This gives you the time to go get clarification from the teacher— before the test.

Sign Up and Soar

The Bible (the number-one best-selling book of all time) says that God has *not* given us a spirit of fear! He has given us His spirit, which fills us with love, equips us with power, and even supplies us with a sound mind (see 2 Timothy 1:7).

Yet have you ever noticed at school that you let fear hold you back? Maybe you're too shy to raise your hand in biology class (even when you're positive you know the answer). Maybe you are afraid of joining the forensics team because you'd be up in front of people and you are too self-conscious about your clothes, your looks, or your new braces. Maybe you want to sign up for auto mechanics, but you know you'd be in the minority. *Stop right there, young lady!*

If you are struggling with fear, it is not from God! It is that ugly enemy rearing his ugly head. He's trying to rock your confidence. Don't let him do it! God has given you a sound mind—you have unlimited learning potential. God has given you power—you can overcome fear of the unknown. Best of all, God has given you love! (You will need it to forgive the guy who tries to intimidate you or the girl who just dissed you. This is one of those really opportune times to look past a person's faults and see his or her *need!*)

If God has put a desire in your heart to do something, go for it! It may not be smooth sailing, but with the Holy Spirit as the wind beneath your wings, you can soar, girlfriend!

You can soar!

Little Hint

Set your goals high and work to achieve them—and never be afraid of failure, for the tragedy comes not from failing, but in never having tried to excel.

Rosalynn Carter, First Lady 1977-1981

Watching Your Rep

The Bible, the most practical book you'll ever study, says: "If you must choose, take a good name rather than great riches; for to be held in loving esteem is better than silver and gold" (Proverbs 22:1).

A good name!

That means a good reputation!

Your reputation is based on your character: who you are, what you do, whom you hang out with, and what kinds of things you do or don't do. It's that "attitude and actions" thing!

My husband's mom, Nell, knew how valuable a good and honorable reputation would be to her kids when they were teens. When Bill was headed out the door for his big football game or softball tournament, an important date, or just a night out with the guys, his mom would say, "Now, Bill, remember who you are and to whom you belong." Nell wasn't trying to lay a guilt trip on her son; she was simply reminding him that he was her son and belonged to a family that was good, hardworking, and well-respected in the community. More important, she was reminding Bill that he was first and foremost a Christian, that he belonged to his heavenly Father, and that he needed to be representing God by controlling his conduct and selecting the right friends and activities.

The same lesson applies to all Christians. If you get mixed up in the wrong crowd or activities, you'll ruin your reputation, shaming your own name. A good reputation is a hard thing to earn back, once it is tainted.

Yes, I know these teen years are a time to test your wings and find out what life is all about. Yet beware. Be selective. Be wise. Be mindful of the fact you are representing your Lord.

Little Hint

The Beach Boys' song "Be True to Your School" has been popular for generations. Take an inventory of your school. What are its special features, best teachers, most enjoyable activities? Why do you appreciate your school and want to be true to it? Having a positive school spirit makes those hallways and classrooms a better place to be!

Cool School Hair

Let's face it, school is like the premier showing of a new movie. It's the place where some teens show up sporting their new look—be it clothes, makeup, glasses, shoes, or yes, hair. The hallways are really runways of the latest trends in hair wear!

Ever get tempted to get in on the action and transform a dull 'do into something totally hip? Before you take that trendy turn, consider the look that's best for you by asking yourself these questions:

1. Is my hair type capable of achieving the style I want?
2. Does this style match my personality (bubbly, sophisticated, or sporty)?
3. Does my lifestyle lend itself to a quick style or a more decorative 'do?
4. Is this style suitable to my wardrobe (classic, contemporary, or trendy)?
5. Is this hairstyle in proportion to my height and weight?

Now check out your face shape. Steer clear of repeating your face shape with your hairstyle. If you have a round, full face, stay away from a super curly and short style. Try a longer, straighter look. If you have a square face, keep curls or fullness away from the corners of your forehead and jaw line. Have an oblong face? No prob! Wear your fullness at the cheekbone. Is your face pear-shaped? Go for wavy or curls on your forehead and smoothness at your jaw line. Is it heart-shaped? Save your fullness for your chin area! Balance is the key to having the best 'do for you!

De-Stress Your School Mess

Stuff happens.

Your locker jams. You drop your books in front of "him." You have broccoli in your braces. Your chair gets pulled away and you land on the floor. You raise your hand and give the wrong answer. You forget about the Spanish test. You wear your shirt inside out. You never have your mom or dad sign your permission slip. You get detention for three tardies in a row.

Stuff happens. Stressful stuff.

You can de-stress your school mess with these six valuable steps:

1. *Detangle your day.* Calmly think through the events of the day or a particular event that went haywire. Sort it out, and identify and address the issue at hand. It always helps to know exactly what you are dealing with!

2. *Analyze your audience.* Do things seem worse because you were trying to impress or please someone? Is there some peer pressure involved? That will always get things mixed up. There are only two smiling faces for which you are responsible ... yours and God's!

3. *Fix what's fixable.* Is there a situation you can do something about? Fix it! Do it. Ask for a makeup test, do extra credit, apologize where needed—whatever! Sometimes you just can't seem to do anything to change or correct a situation. In that case, let it be. Pray about it. Invite God right into the situation to help you work it out.

4. *Brush off the yucky stuff.* If something rotten happens (you flunked a test, you dropped a glob of jelly on your new shirt, a friend broke your confidence), be honest and acknowledge that it was awful, then tell yourself, "I'm letting this go; I'm moving on." Make it a conscious choice.

5. *Find the funny side.* When you get past the initial sting or shock of

a stressful situation, you can usually find something totally funny about it. Look for it. It's there!

6. *Put it in perspective.* Ask yourself, "Do I *really* want to let this wreck my day?" "Will this matter ten years from now?" A little perspective can de-stress *any* mess!

Little Hint

When homework, sports, college applications, clubs, or a job threaten to take over your life, *simplify, simplify, simplify!* Ask yourself: What is really important? What could be eliminated? What are the "necessary" things? What is the "good part" I don't want to miss? Keep what's important and get rid of the riffraff!

What's in Your Backpack?

Pull it off your shoulders, set it down, and zip it open! Now take a peek inside. Look deeper. What's in your backpack? What attitudes are you carrying around with you on campus?

Here are the attitudes God wants you to have filling your backpack and shining through your life. Read each definition and do some soul-searching. On a scale of 1 to 10, where do you stand on each of these 'tudes?

Attitude of Love
To unconditionally love others, even if they have been unloving to you. Not being selfish and rude.

Attitude of Joy
To show joy, even when life is crumbling around you, trusting that God is in control. Not being depressed or grumpy.

Attitude of Peace

To be worry-free, content, and trusting God, even if you don't have all the answers. Not being totally stressed out.

Attitude of Patience

To remain calm and willing to wait even where there is pressure. Not demanding instant action.

Attitude of Kindness

To be tenderhearted, showing mercy and forgiveness toward others, even if they have mistreated you. Not being mean and revengeful.

Attitude of Goodness

To practice moral values even when others say, "If it feels good, do it." Not being deceitful.

Attitude of Faithfulness

To follow through and not grow weary in your well-doing, even when you are tempted to quit. Not giving in and not giving up.

Attitude of Meekness

To show humility and boast in the Lord, not yourself. Not being cocky and self-reliant.

Attitude of Self-Control

To show inward strength, refraining from doing or saying things that would not please the Lord. Not being ruled by temptations.

As you yield your life to the Holy Spirit, these attitudes will become evident. They are the fruit of God's Spirit in you. Though it is His job to produce these attitudes, you can certainly help or hinder His progress. You can choose to work with the Holy Spirit or to dig in your heels and refuse.

So, take these positive attitudes with you to school every day. They will help you, and those around you, to have a better day!

Hanging Out

Is your social life being squeezed by your special talents? Listen up!

Kelly was introduced to gymnastics when her mom enrolled her in Tumblin' Toddlers, a class for four-year-olds at the local community center. It was love at first somersault! Kelly started private training in grade school. Her coordination, skill, and graceful control were evident. Kelly earned high scores at local, regional, and state gymnastic meets. She was a natural. Her coaches were well aware of her abilities and were preparing her step-by-step for the U.S. Olympic team.

Yet when Kelly was in junior high, a snag in the plans came up. She had spent many years and thousands of hours polishing routines and perfecting moves. Those were precious hours, but they could have been spent with her friends. Kelly missed out on football games, class dances, church camp, and sleepovers, all because she had to stay fine-tuned for her competitive sport. When Kelly couldn't go on the eighth-grade graduation trip because of a state meet, however, she had had it. She wanted to be free to hang out with her friends at the mall or go to the movies without worrying about getting home early on Friday nights for Saturday's workout or competition. The pressure Kelly was getting from her parents and coaches not to quit made her more determined to do whatever she wanted.

What Kelly interpreted as pressure was really justified concern. The coaches didn't want Kelly to quit gymnastics and waste her God-given talent just to hang out with her friends.

I've known many girls like Kelly. Marcie excelled on the keyboard, Lindsey in drawing, and Maggie in ballet. Each of them shelved their talent for the sake of their social life. They just wanted time to hang! To be idle.

Kelly and the others may have felt that their practice schedule was cheating them out of some fun times. Yet, in the long run, who gets cheated?

For one, God does. If a person has exceptional natural abilities, they are a blessed gift from God. He wants that person to develop and use the talent for Him. Being idle is not God's plan for His children. Perhaps God's plan for Kelly was to be a witness for Him on the women's U.S. Olympic team. Maybe a special spot was prepared for Marcie to play in a Christian band. If we ignore our talents, are we being unfair to God?

Second, many girls don't know the real feeling of being cheated until they realize that they have temporarily followed the wrong path for their lives. Thoughts of what they could have accomplished have plagued people for centuries.

Hangin' out, sitting around with too much time on your hands is OK for a while. Yet when kids aren't pursuing their interests and talents, extra time becomes idle. Idle time has driven many teens straight to juvenile hall. They come up with stuff to do to fill their time, but the wrong kind of stuff!

What about you? Do you have a talent that you're ignoring? Does the self-discipline seem too tough? Are you wasting time, coasting through life? Will you be one of the millions who look back with nothing but wasted days and wasted nights to show for their teen years, because all they wanted to do was "hang out"? Give it some thought. Discover, uncover, or recover that gift God has planted in you!

> *God has given each of you some special abilities; be sure to use them to help each other, passing on to others God's many kinds of blessings.*
>
> 1 PETER 4:10

Leave a Legacy on Campus

Some Tips for Impacting Your School for Christ
From Katie Pretzel, BRIO Girl 2002

To Leave a Legacy: To make a mark. To be remembered for your stance, your beliefs. To leave a lifelong impression on all those who encounter you. To have a passion to be different and unique. To be completely true to yourself and to what God has called you to be.

Leaving a legacy in your very own school is one of the most important things you are called to do. In other words, I believe God has called each and every one of us to make a mark, to help change our campuses, to be a light for Him (see Matthew 5:14-16). It all starts with being a witness for Him. A witness is one who has seen or had an experience and lives to tell others about it. A witness is one whose life serves as evidence or proof of his or her inner convictions and beliefs. So, being a Christian witness means living your life in such a way that others watching will know you believe in, live for, and love God!

When we make God the foundation of our lives, it is really not that hard to stand up for Him. Yes, you are in high school (or maybe junior high), and yes, there are many trials and temptations facing you, but if you have a true desire to be a witness for God, He will give you the strength to hold true to your morals and beliefs (see Joshua 1:9).

I believe it is important for us to be witnesses for God because we could potentially be the only Bible some people ever read (see 2 Corinthians 3:2-3). Our actions are what they see, and our words are what they hear (see Ephesians 4:29). All of these things add up to what they believe a Christian is like. I encourage you to live a life that represents Christ to the best of your ability.

Are you wondering how you can be a bold witness at your school?

First, start with your reputation. How do people see you? What are you known for? Do you hang with teens who bring out the best in you and believe the same things you do? (You can get a glimpse of someone's personality and values by the company he or she keeps.) Do you buckle under peer pressure or hold true to your convictions?

Second, get involved in a school Bible study. There are many different organizations that sponsor campus Bible studies, like Youth for Christ (Campus Life), and FCA (Fellowship of Christian Athletes, fca.org). If you don't have a Bible study or Bible club on campus, start one! Get a few friends together, then ask a teacher or faculty member to be part of an early morning study (or prayer group) that you hold once a week before school. Your actions and passions will ignite a flame not only in yourself, but in the people around you as well (see 1 Timothy 4:12).

Third, be yourself and live for God—no matter what other people say or do! Fully and wholeheartedly give your life to Him and see what amazing things He does with you right there at your school. He will use you in ways you never thought possible, if you allow Him to!

So, be brave, be bold, be a witness for God on your campus! Make an impact for Him that will serve as your legacy!

The Top 20 Countdown

Give these witnessing tips a try! Trust the Lord and see what happens! Make it a spiritual adventure!

1. Keep a tight relationship with the Lord, so others will see and hear a difference in you!
2. Refuse to cuss. Make up corny words if you have to, just don't swear.

3. Dress in a way that honors God—nothing revealing or alluring to the guys.

4. Use opportunities to share your beliefs—class papers, projects, and speeches.

5. Stop gossip. Question the truth of rumors and hearsay.

6. Don't cheat on tests or copy a friend's homework.

7. Speak the truth instead of falling into the lying trap.

8. Attend or start a campus Bible club and "See You at the Pole." (Check out www.syatp.com.)

9. Keep your virginity. Wear a purity ring and tell people what it means to you.

10. Treat others fairly. Be kind. Be patient. Be loving.

11. Don't freak over things—trust God with whatever is happening.

12. Offer to pray for classmates. Check back with them later to see how they're doing.

13. Invite others to your church and youth group.

14. Don't laugh at cruel jokes or put-downs.

15. Start conversations with classmates about faith and about God.

16. Use current books, songs, and movies to bring up Christian themes or principles.

17. Don't go to parties, and don't drink alcohol or use drugs.

18. Carry your Bible or devotional book to school—it's a definite conversation starter.

19. Pause to pray before you eat lunch.

20. Look people in the eye and smile. That alone will let others know there is something different about you. A light that is shining from the inside out!

Katie Pretzel is the 2002 BRIO Girl. She is a high school senior from Plymouth, Minnesota, who loves pottery, Rollerblading, and receiving mail! She is an FCA leader on her campus.

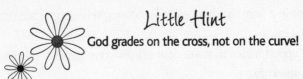

Little Hint
God grades on the cross, not on the curve!

Rumors Ringing From the Halls

She got in line at the checkout stand and was taken in by the headlines. Mindy confessed that she was curious, so she went for it! Her hand just reached out and grabbed them. The *Star,* the *Globe,* the *Inquirer, People* Magazine. Then her mind got in on the action. The more she read, the more she wanted to keep reading.

It pulled her in like some cyber-force.

Then she reached the checkout counter and did the unthinkable. She actually paid money for them—her hard-earned baby-sitting money. Was three hours of changing dirty diapers worth the exchange? She pushed the question out of her mind as she let the latest new gossip in.

Inquiring minds want to know!

That's what they say, anyway.

Yet, wanting to *know* leads to wanting to *tell.* When someone has just dished out the baddest buzz about someone, it is hard to hold it in. Yet getting the lowdown on someone and passing it on can leave that person feeling low and down. (You know what I mean, because it has probably happened to you!)

Spreading gossip can cause someone else to have a bummer of a day. So when you hear a rumor ringing in the halls at your school, only pass it on if it is good news!

Be discreet! Don't repeat!

A gossip goes around spreading rumors, while a trustworthy man [or woman] tries to quiet them.

PROVERBS 11:13

Semester Finals

It happens once each semester ... finals! The time when worry and stress can kick into high gear. The time when you cram your brain to the brim. The time when you pull all-nighters in hopes of pulling off passing grades.

Prevent a total meltdown by keeping this stuff in mind:

♥ Don't procrastinate. (It prolongs the inevitable—the test is coming, ready or not!)

♥ Work a little at a time. (It eases the pressure of cramming and makes you less tense.)

♥ Get rid of distractions. (Go for solitude so you can do some serious concentrating.)

♥ Plan a study group. (After you've studied alone, get with a group to benefit from their insight and explanations.)

♥ Make flashcards or self-tests. (This can really help with memorizing the material.)

♥ Review old tests. (They may be a good indicator of what will be on the final.)

♥ Keep it in perspective. (Finals are usually about 20 percent of your semester grade.)

♥ Pray. (Ask God to bless your memory, give you peace, and help you persevere to do your best.)

Little Hint

Want to be voted "most likely to succeed"? Follow God's formula to success:

This book of the law shall not depart from your mouth, but you shall meditate on it day and night, so that you may be careful to do according to all that is written in it; for then you will make your way prosperous, and then you will have success.

JOSHUA 1:8, NAS

Study God's Word! Keep God's guidelines in the forefront of your heart and mind. Apply them and you will have the TRUE success!

Graduation Day

Finally, the big event you've dreamed about during those boring history lectures: graduation! You polish your class ring against the shiny polyester grad gown. It's almost your big moment. Straightening your cap, you walk across the stage. The principal gives your hand a strong shake as you take your diploma. Dad flashes the camera and sighs with relief. Mom wipes a tear from her eye. You reach up to your tassel, moving it from one side to the other. The official declaration of your accomplishment. You did it!

Returning to your seat, the questions, the panic, and the fears rise to form a lump in your throat. *What now?*

The options may seem too big and too varied. You may feel overwhelmed at the idea of what lies around the next curve in your life. Some teens feel all alone in a sea of indecision at this point in their journey. Do you?

Fear not! God has a plan, He's always with you, and He wants you to know what He wants for your life. Stay close to Him, seek Him in prayer, and He will show you each step.

When it comes to a specific career, prayerfully consider the following:

♥ *What are you naturally good at?* Has God gifted you in a special area: music, sports, organization, math, science, working with children or the elderly? God-given talents and abilities are often an indication of the direction He wants you to go.

♥ *What are your hobbies and interests?* It's important to do something you enjoy. Too many people have spent half their lives at jobs they hate (it may pay more or please a parent, but what a drag)!

♥ *What is your definition of success?* How you answer this question will affect the decisions you make. John the Baptist was no success in the world's eyes. He lived in the woods, ate locusts, and was beheaded in his early thirties! Yet he had fulfilled God's plan for his life. God considered his life a success. Do you think fame and fortune are the name of the game, or do character, integrity, and obedience to God rank higher for you? Do you agree that true success is finding out what God wants you to do, and doing it?

No matter the profession to which you hear God calling you, do it to the best of your ability and for His glory! Your shining example will attract the attention of others. It may open the door for you to share Christ with them. *That* you can do no matter where you work or what you do!

The Future? No Worries!

Here are four solid reasons you can trust God and not worry about the future. Look up each Scripture passage and rewrite it in your own words.

God loves you (see 1 John 4:9-10)

_____

_____

_____

God is always with you (see Hebrews 13:5-6)

_____

_____

_____

God is at work in your life (see Philippians 1:6; 2:13)

_____

_____

_____

God will give you what you need to do His will (see Hebrews 13:20-21)

_____

_____

_____

Fear robs you of the joy in life. Read 1 John 4:18 to find out what God's perfect love does to fear. How does God want you to respond, the next time you feel fearful?

_____

_____

God does not want you to worry! Find out what you are to do instead. Read Philippians 4:6-7 and write out God's blueprint for peace!

_____

_____

_____

Financing Your College Dream
Some Sweet Advice About Scholarships From Stephanie C. Inks

Dreams Come True

I remember the evening I knelt beside my violet-and-white-colored bedspread and asked God to provide the money for college. I knew my family didn't have the financial resources to pay for my education at a private university, and I was philosophically opposed to loans. Of course, my heavenly Father also knew this. I decided that winter night of 1997 that I would do all I could to make a way for college and to trust God with the results.

With the help and support of my family, I worked countless hours over the next year and a half on over three dozen scholarship applications. Let there be no doubt, however, that it was only the grace of God that gave me close to $100,000 in scholarships for my undergraduate study. Praise be to Him who is able to do more than all we can possibly dream or imagine (see Ephesians 3:20).

Do you have dreams of going to college and don't know how you are ever going to get there? If you are willing to work harder than you have ever worked before, and have faith in God, then continue to read. I hope this information is the beginning of an exciting new path for you!

Positioning Yourself

The most important aspect of earning scholarships is what you do with yourself between your freshman and senior years of high school. In order to impress a scholarship committee, you should have a solid record in community service, academics, S.A.T. or A.C.T. scores, leadership roles and honors, and what I will call "your niche." It is also important to remember, however, that there are scholarships of *all different kinds* just waiting to be won ... the secret is preparing early and applying!

Community service is usually the heart of the scholarship application. Most of the major scholarships require you to list all of your service activities, including the dates and hours you donated for each. Some require you to write essays about your most meaningful volunteer experience. I suggest you start by volunteering a few hours every week and build up a strong record of service to your community (remember to keep a detailed log of your activity, including the date, the hours, the title of the project, and the name of a supervisor).

Next, you *really need to study!* While it may be obvious that the higher your G.P.A. is, the better your application, it is also important to remember that committees are usually interested in your class rank. Since rank is often determined by just fractions of points, you should pay close attention to your grades and strive to do your very best! Do extra credit when possible.

Perhaps the *toughest* aspect of your application is your standardized test scores (designed to measure students by using the same standard). Most researchers and educators agree that serious study for these tests *can* significantly improve your results. Truth is, the reason these scores are so hard to improve is because most students lack the motivation to study seriously for them. I recommend studying a few hours a week for about four months before you take the exam (you could even join a study group and make it fun). You can find plenty of helpful (and sometimes free) resources on the Internet and at bookstores. Challenge yourself to take the tests at least twice, if not more (but remember, each time you take it, it goes on your record).

Almost every scholarship committee is looking for leaders. In order to shine on paper, you need to have some leadership experience under your belt. Run for a class office. Start a service group or other club. Serve as editor of the school newspaper (if you don't have one, don't be afraid to start one). There are so many opportunities!

Lastly, figure out what your niche is. Where does most of your potential lie? What activity do you love the most? Perhaps it is a sport, music or art, debate or forensics. What topics interest you? History, business, or journalism? For me, it was politics and public policy. Whatever it is, get involved and excel in it. When it comes time to fill out those applications, you will have a well-rounded personality waiting to break through.

Do Your Research

You could drown in an ocean of scholarship research if you don't know how to swim the waters properly. I found www.fastweb.com to be the most beneficial service for finding scholarships ... and ironically, it is free! Instead of spending hours searching page after page in books that make your phone book look skinny, you can spend an hour filling out an application on fastweb. After that, you will receive a personal profile of scholarships for which you are eligible and links to their home pages. After receiving my personal profile, I went to each of the scholarship home pages and printed out all of the information I could get my hands on regarding each scholarship. For some, I had to send a letter via postal mail requesting an application along with an SASE (self-addressed, stamped envelope). Then, I organized my information according to the application deadlines in a huge, three-ring binder. It is important to pay very close attention to the deadlines. For example, some applications must be *received* by January 15, and others must be *postmarked* by January 15. Unlike your gracious English teacher, these committees will not grant you extensions ... so make sure you don't miss a deadline!

Preparation Time

From the envelope to the essay, your scholarship application should be as close to perfect as possible. Starting the night before a deadline will almost certainly ensure your application's fatality. Some applications require official transcripts, signatures, and other documentation. Most require essays of some kind, and *all* require your best efforts.

When you are completing the application form, use a typewriter, and when writing the essays, use a computer. Always make sure that you follow every instruction. Neglecting to do so could get your hours of hard work disqualified in a few seconds. Some committees will even disqualify you for stapling your materials improperly! The key is to read all of the instructions carefully before you begin, once you are engaged in your work, and again before you mail it. When in doubt about an instruction, call the foundation or organization and ask!

Your essays are vital to your application because they reveal your character and personality. Through them you will show the judges whether you are serious-minded, witty, intelligent, articulate, or committed. The only sure way to have a great essay is to write, rewrite, have someone else (such as a trusted teacher) critique it, and then write it again. Sometimes committees request letters of recommendation. It is usually best to ask someone (besides family members and peers) who knows you very well both inside and outside the classroom. Remember to give your reference at least a month's notice and to thank him or her with a note when he or she is finished.

If allowed, spice up your application with a professional-looking portfolio and send along articles you have written, newspaper clippings of your achievements, and photographs of your service projects.

Let It Go

After hours, days, and even weeks of hard work, you must surrender your application to God's will. I struggled (and still do) to lay down my dreams before Christ. Every time I sent in an application, my parents and I prayed, "Lord, this belongs to You. I pray that it will find favor in the sight of man, according to Your will." Most of all, we continued to pray for each application. Ultimately, peace is found when you trust the One who holds the future—your future—in the palm of His gentle hand.

Stephanie C. Inks is a student at Hillsdale College, where she will graduate with degrees in philosophy, history, and Spanish. Stephanie directs a mentoring program for kids, speaks on abstinence for Project Reality, directs the college's mime team, and writes for the college newspaper.

Grades 'n Stuff Finale

Buzzz!

Tell the truth. When your morning alarm goes off, are you filled with elated enthusiasm or annoying anxiety? Does apprehension or anticipation flow through your veins as you step into the shower to prepare for school?

Take note. How you answer those questions can affect whether the 200 or so days a year that you spend sitting in class, preparing projects, taking tests, and milling through the cafeteria, are good days or crummy days.

See, this chapter gets you headed in a positive direction. You are now learning to organize yourself, make the most of your time, deal with the big and little stresses, improve your grades, and plan for your post-grad days, but really, outlook is (almost) everything.

So, which is it for you? Elated enthusiasm or annoying anxiety? If you are falling closer to anxiety, check yourself. What attitudes do you need to change? Does your schedule need to be adjusted to make you a happier kind of girl?

Depending on whether you are a frosh, soph, junior, or senior, you still have years of school ahead of you.

You can make the grade.

Make 'em great!

It's a Wrap!

So there you have it, my friend. A whole book filled with stuff you've gotta know. Yes, it only scratches the surface, but it gets you well on your way to being clued in on girl stuff, growing up stuff, girlfriend stuff, God stuff, guy stuff, and grades 'n stuff.

My prayer is that you will seek God's guidance as you maneuver your way through the stuff of life. As you turn to Him, He will lead you in this wonderful, incredible journey known as the life of a teenage girl! Many blessings to you!

Leader's Guide Info

Hey, why not gather up a few of your friends and go through this book together? You can put together a group, I know you can! Or perhaps you are reading this and you are a youth leader or a mom who wants her daughter to have the opportunity to chat through these topics with other teen girls. Great!

I have created a brief leader's guide that is easy to use no matter your age or experience level. You can find it on my website. Just go to www.andreastephens.com and click on Books 'n Stuff. Find *Stuff a Girl's Gotta Know*, then click on Leader's Guide! There it is! May God bless you as you invest your time in teens!

The BABE Seminar

God thinks you're a BABE!

Andrea will prove it in this fun, upbeat seminar designed especially for teen girls!

Listen while Andrea chats with you and your friends about these great topics!

Learn to **LOVE** Your Look!
Your **Bod** is a Gift From God!
Passionate **Purity!**
Unbelievable Beauty From the **INSIDE** Out!

For more information about The BABE Seminar contact:

Andrea Stephens

P.O. Box 2856

Bakersfield, CA 93303

Or check out her website at:

www.andreastephens.com

It's a great idea for your youth outreach event, retreat,
camp, or luncheon at your church
or school!